LAST DAYS OF THE HIGH FLIER

Dennis J Reardon

BROADWAY PLAY PUBLISHING INC
New York
www.broadwayplaypublishing.com
info@broadwayplaypublishing.com

LAST DAYS OF THE HIGH FLIER
© Copyright 2004 by Dennis J Reardon

Cover art by Jeff Rosenplot, Rosenplot Design
First printing: November 2004
I S B N: 978-0-88145-250-1

Book design: Marie Donovan
Word processing: Microsoft Word
Typographic controls: Xerox Ventura Publisher 2.0 P E
Typeface: Palatino
Printed and bound in the U S A

LAST DAYS OF THE HIGH FLIER premiered at the
Ruth N Halls Theater in the Lee Norvelle Theater and
Drama Center of Indiana University in Bloomington, IN
on 27 February 2004. The cast and creative contributors
were:

KEVIN . . . . Josh Gaboian
CLYDE . . . . Mike Mauloff
FOGARTY . . . . .Brendan Pentzell
FRANCIS GARY POWERS . . . . Andy Higgins
PHIPPS . . . . Phil Kasper
DARLA . . . . Meg Cionni
JOANNA . . . . Christina Pumariega
NURSE/P L . . . . Maysee Yang Herr
ORDERLY*/N V A . . . . Peter Quach
LIBRARIAN* . . . . Jessica Krueger
CHARLIE* . . . . David Charles
CHRISTINA* . . . . Renee Racan

Director . . . . Dale McFadden
Scenic design . . . . Edward Haynes
Costume design . . . . Staci Kern
Lighting and sound design . . . . C C Conn

*Roles marked with * have been eliminated in this published
version. In addition, it is no longer recommended that the
Pathet Lao (P L) soldier be doubled with the NURSE.*

I am indebted to that entire cast and crew of the Indiana
University production, and in particular to director
Dale McFadden for championing the play script.

CHARACTERS & SETTING

KEVIN O'ROURKE; *twenty*
CLYDE; *twenty*
FRED FOGARTY; *about thirty-seven (Freddy the Fog; Frog)*
DARLA; *twenty*
PHIPPS; *fortyish or older*
JOANNA BRADY; *twenty*
FRANCIS GARY POWERS; *about thirty-seven*
NURSE
Two soldiers: a North Vietnamese Army (N V A) regular a Pathet Lao (P L) guerrilla

Time: The main action of the play occurs from June 1963 through New Year's Eve 1963. Not infrequently specific dates during this time-frame are cited. A small portion of the play depicts events taking place in Laos in 1961, and a few scenes suggest a moment happening in Moscow on August 11, 1960.

Place: Primarily a college town in eastern Kansas. Also, a mental hospital in Topeka; a mountain trail near the Plain of Jars in Laos; a prison cell in Moscow.

Sets: Suffice to say here that fluidity is the key in a multiple scene play such as this. Recommend a multilevel unit set with props and lighting suggesting specific playing areas, the most important of which are KEVIN's apartment, FOGARTY's apartment, a pier overlooking a lake, and an alcove in the corridor of an academic building.

SCENOGRAPHY

Scene One: Bluebell Lake
Scene Two: Alcove in a campus corridor
Scene Three: Kevin's apartment
Scene Four: The Emergency Room
Scene Five: Bluebell Lake
Scene Six: Alcove in a campus corridor
Scene Seven: Kevin's apartment
Scene Eight: Fogarty's apartment and a jail cell in
Moscow

ACT TWO

Scene Nine: Topeka State Hospital
Scene Ten: Library carrel and a jail cell in Moscow
Scene Eleven: Kevin's apartment
Scene Twelve: Fogarty's apartment, Laos, Moscow
Scene Thirteen: Fogarty's apartment
Scene Fourteen: Fogarty's apartment
Scene Fifteen: Topeka State Hospital
Scene Sixteen: Alcove in a campus corridor
Scene Seventeen: Kevin's apartment
Scene Eighteen: Bluebell Lake

About suffering they were never wrong,
The Old Masters: how well they understood
Its human position; how it takes place
While someone else is eating or opening a window or
    just walking dully along...

In Brueghel's *Icarus*, for instance: how everything turns
    away
Quite leisurely from the disaster; the plowman may
Have heard the splash, the forsaken cry,
But for him it was not an important failure; the sun
    shone
As it had to on the white legs disappearing into the
    green
Water; and the expensive delicate ship that must have
    seen
Something amazing, a boy falling out of the sky,
Had somewhere to get to and sailed calmly on.

from W H Auden's Musee des Beaux Arts

Special thanks to Mary; Dale Regier; Dr Tom Sharp;
Charlotte and Marty Stradtman; Gen Vang Pao and the
Hmong people of Laos; and to Patrick S, wherever life
led you.

for my mother and my father with
gratitude and love

ACT ONE
WHEATLAND

Scene One
The Pier, Bluebell Lake

(June 1963. A pier overlooking Bluebell Lake in the countryside near a Kansas college town. It's around midnight under a full moon. Two twenty year old boys are sprawled on the dock, trying to catch a breeze in the sticky summer heat. CLYDE is a big athletic kid; he's drinking beer. His friend KEVIN is working on something from a pint bottle. They seem deep in contemplation.)

KEVIN: Do you think there's really any such thing as a nymphomaniac?

CLYDE: Not around here.

KEVIN: Just something they dreamed up to make us feel even worse.

CLYDE: Still haven't sealed the deal with Darla, huh?

KEVIN: I'm dying on the vine, Clyde.

CLYDE: What're you gonna do? They don't wanna get pregnant.

KEVIN: I heard they had a pill for that.

CLYDE: Yeah, that'll be the day. Hey, that reminds me, my dad just got a letter from the Board of Education. They're thinking about teaching sex in school, and they want him on the committee looking into it.

KEVIN: Your dad? *(Beat)* Maybe they want to guarantee at least one "No" vote.

CLYDE: My fear is the other committee members are hoping Dad can explain it all to them.

KEVIN: Yeah. "First, you turn off all the lights..."

CLYDE: Listen to us. Laughing to keep from crying. Kevin, we can't even be sure sex exists.

KEVIN: Sure it does. In Sweden.

CLYDE: Is that why you keep dragging my ass off to Bergman movies? *(Beat)* I don't get that guy.

KEVIN: You liked *The Seventh Seal.*

CLYDE: The Grim Reaper was cool. *(Beat) From Russia With Love.* Now that's a flick.

(CLYDE starts doing the theme from that Bond movie)

CLYDE: Da da dee dah, dee dah dah...

(KEVIN joins him for a couple bars, but he's not looking well.)

CLYDE & KEVIN: Da da dee dah, dee dah dah...

(KEVIN stretches over the edge of the pier, preferably head out of sight, and retches. CLYDE takes it in stride. KEVIN pulls himself together.)

KEVIN: What goes down, must come up.

CLYDE: What was tonight's emetic?

KEVIN: Apricot-flavored brandy.

CLYDE: God, why do you do this to yourself? What's wrong with beer?

KEVIN: I want to become more sophisticated.

CLYDE: *(Beat)* People drink from Bluebell Lake. And you puking in it every Friday night?

KEVIN: Clyde...fish piss in it, people drown in it—

CLYDE: Oh, so you heard about the body?

KEVIN: Somebody drowned?

CLYDE: You didn't hear all those sirens around
two-thirty? They found it right off the point,
right out there.

KEVIN: Please tell me it was Donnie Cox I hate that
phony pseudo.

CLYDE: Turned out to be a dead carp.

KEVIN: A fish?

CLYDE: Big one. Belly up.

KEVIN: *(Beat)* Nothing ever happens around here.

CLYDE: I'm thinking of doing my column on it in the
Daily Stupid tomorrow. I'm stuck on a headline. I can't
decide between "Murder Most Carp" or "Car-pe Diem."

KEVIN: Don't ask me. I just puked. *(Beat)* Wait...got it.
"Belly-Up at Blueballs Lake."

(CLYDE *regards him with some approval and so signifies by
gently clinking his beer bottle against* KEVIN's *brow.)*

KEVIN: You see that picture in The Star this morning?
The one with the Negro lady in the pretty dress?

CLYDE: In handcuffs? Yeah. You see the sub-head?
"Eleven Arrested. Nine of them were Negroes." *(Beat)*
Classy.

KEVIN: Yeah. Nine for their side, two for ours.

CLYDE: Does that mean we're winning or losing?

KEVIN: She was dressed like she was going to church,
like for her daughter's wedding. The way she was
covering her face just made the handcuffs so obvious.
I felt bad for her.

CLYDE: Well, they shouldn't have been smoking marijuana.

KEVIN: No, apparently not, Clyde. You unforgiving twerp.

CLYDE: The law's the law.

KEVIN: Every time you open one of those beers you're breaking a law.

CLYDE: *Touché.*

KEVIN: I wonder what it does to you.

CLYDE: Marijuana? Makes you see bright lights. That's what I hear.

KEVIN: There's got to be more to it than that. Don't you think? If it's nothing more than that, why are they arresting that lady?

CLYDE: And why would she risk being arrested?

KEVIN: Exactly. *(Beat)* There's something going on there. *(Beat)* I wonder how I could get some.

CLYDE: I think you have to ask a Negro.

KEVIN: Yeah? You know any?

CLYDE: I played ball with some. Lost touch.

KEVIN: I'll bet James Dean smoked marijuana.

CLYDE: Yeah. Right before he totaled his Porsche. Why do you want to be a junkie anyway?

KEVIN: Clyde, it's got to be better for you than this fucking apricot-flavored brandy. *(Beat)* You ever wish you were a Negro?

CLYDE: Not really. Do you?

KEVIN: Sometimes. They look like they have interesting lives.

CLYDE: If they lived here they wouldn't.

KEVIN: Truth. Verily.

(They stare at the lake for a few moments, then wearily exit. Scene)

Scene Two
Alcove, Wheatland University

(Lights up on a small alcove in a corridor within an academic building on the campus of Wheatland University. It's a student recreational area—pleasant enough with fake shrubbery and a short ledge or bench. Sort of messy: soft drink cups, sand-filled ashtray, etc. Enter FRED FOGARTY. *He carries a ratty briefcase in one hand and a cup of coffee in the other. He is slightly-built and in his late-thirties. He is respectably dressed but seems thread-bare, maybe even slovenly. He settles in, takes some pills from his briefcase, washes them down with his coffee.* KEVIN *enters. He wears a short-sleeved dark blue shirt with his name above a pocket. He's working as a janitor to pay his tuition, and his props should say that—perhaps a wheeled barrel into which he dumps the assorted empty cups; certainly a small "sifter" used to clean butts from the ashtray sand. As* KEVIN *goes about his menial tasks, he becomes uncomfortably aware of* FOGARTY *intensely observing him. When he glances over,* FOGARTY *grins at him and lifts his coffee cup as if proposing a toast.)*

FOGARTY: You're a good worker. Scrupulous.

KEVIN: All I'm doing is taking cigarette butts out of an ashtray.

FOGARTY: All of 'em! Got 'em all! Thorough.

*(*KEVIN *smiles politely, goes back to work.)*

FOGARTY: You're the son of a good man.

KEVIN: What?

FOGARTY: Kind of guy wants to make the old man proud. I know the type. I am one, darned if I'm not. *(He emits an odd little laugh as if he's just told a good one on himself.)*

KEVIN: You know my father?

FOGARTY: Brilliant lecturer—caring, humane.

KEVIN: Oh. You took a class from him.

FOGARTY: Three.

KEVIN: Three?

FOGARTY: My favorite was Political Decision Making. Amazing use of Game Theory overlaid on Geopolitics. You ever take a class from him, Kevin?

KEVIN: No, I...how do you know my name?

FOGARTY: *(Pointing)* Shirt pocket, Kevin.

KEVIN: Oh. Yeah. I forget sometimes. So you were one of his grad students?

FOGARTY: Not formally. I'm all over the place. Kind of an Individualized Program sort of thing. *(extends his hand; they shake)* Fogarty. Fred Fogarty. *(The little laugh)* Freddy the Fog. Sometimes just Frog. In certain circles. *(Pause)* You must miss him. Your dad? Going off to Berkeley like that? Must be the first time you've been on your own.

KEVIN: I don't mind.

(Everything about Fogarty makes Kevin uncomfortable. He returns to his custodial tasks, hoping to curtail further conversation. It doesn't work. As FOGARTY rambles on, an older man becomes visible and listens in. This is PHIPPS.)

FOGARTY: Me? I've been catting around on my own since I was fifteen. Ran off and joined the Navy. Lied about my age. Took 'em a while to catch on. Gave me a bus ticket and sent me home. I turned right around and signed up again. Flight School. They couldn't keep me out. Some people spend their whole life wondering what they're supposed to do. Not me, boy, no sir, not Freddy the Fog. Pilot. Born to fly. Always knew it.

PHIPPS: Mister Fogarty.

(FOGARTY *is startled. Approaches* PHIPPS *deferentially, almost timidly.*)

FOGARTY: Sir?

PHIPPS: (*Trying to be amiable, unsuccessfully*) Aren't we keeping you busy enough around here, Mr Fogarty? Got time enough to sit around like a Kentucky Colonel, just yakking with the help?

(PHIPPS *shoots a quick, dismissive glance at* KEVIN, *who is doing his best to ignore them as he works.* FOGARTY's *laugh sounds even more forced than usual around* PHIPPS.)

PHIPPS: How we doing, Freddie? Really? Taking your meds?

FOGARTY: (*Glancing at his watch*) Pretty much on schedule, Dr Phipps, yes sir.

PHIPPS: Health, Freddie. If you've got that, you've got everything.

FOGARTY: Roger that, sir.

PHIPPS: Are you going to need an incomplete?

FOGARTY: I don't believe so, sir.

PHIPPS: I only ask because your last report's two weeks overdue.

FOGARTY: Yes sir, I know, I'm...I'll have it for you by Friday, sir, I promise.

PHIPPS: By noon?

FOGARTY: Can do, sir.

PHIPPS: Looking forward to it. But not at the expense of your sleep, you hear? Health first, work next. Nature's the sternest taskmaster, Mr Fogarty. Obey her imperatives, the rest will follow as the night the day.

FOGARTY: Thank you, sir.

(PHIPPS *exits with a quick glance back that catches* KEVIN *glaring at him.* FOGARTY *seems unnerved; sits, rummages through his briefcase.* KEVIN *watches with some alarm as* FOGARTY *swallows pills from several containers.)*

KEVIN: You're sick?

FOGARTY: Hmm? Oh. Uh, I have a condition.

KEVIN: I hate that man. He's such a dickhead.

FOGARTY: Dr Phipps? He's O K. He's very highly regarded, you know.

KEVIN: What's he to you?

FOGARTY: The Chair of my doctoral committee.

KEVIN: Oh, you poor bastard.

FOGARTY: You don't like authority, do you, Kevin?

KEVIN: I don't pucker up for each passing asshole, no.

(FOGARTY *is feeling the effects of his medication; temporarily loses focus)*

FOGARTY: Chain of Command...

KEVIN: What?

FOGARTY: Great Chain of Being...from God on down to me, from me on down to...the amoeba.

KEVIN: Are you O K?

FOGARTY: Without it, the forces of Chaos are unleashed.

KEVIN: Mr Fogarty, I think you should get on over to the Student Health Clinic.

FOGARTY: Choices. Every day, thousands of choices. We can never know the consequences until they reveal themselves. It's too late then. That's what makes it all so interesting. That's the great mystery at the heart of our lives. *(Beat)* Do you like mysteries, Kevin? Raymond Chandler?

KEVIN: Um, no, not especially.

FOGARTY: No, not serious enough for you. You read Camus. Kafka. Faulkner.

(KEVIN *is a bit taken aback by the specificity and accuracy of that.)*

FOGARTY: You going on to graduate school?

KEVIN: Maybe.

FOGARTY: That's a choice. That would make your dad proud, wouldn't it? Follow in his footsteps? Spend the next eight years writing your dissertation on the size of Faulkner's liver. Maybe get lucky, get some non-tenured posting to some dipshit little community college in Cutoffmyballs, Kansas. Marry some frigid bitch in the Psychology Department. Contemplate suicide for the next forty years. Have your heart attack. Vanish without a trace that you ever existed. That what you want, Kevin?

(KEVIN *is staring at him. A trace of a smile. Listening closely)*

FOGARTY: Your dad told us you want to be a writer. That's a very different choice. It comes down to whether you choose stability...or you choose to be a high flier. Slither around with the snakes, or soar with the eagles.

KEVIN: *(Calmly but warily)* Why are you talking to me?

FOGARTY: We like you, Kevin.

KEVIN: We do?

FOGARTY: You have greatness in you. Let it out. Fly.

KEVIN: What are you saying? Join the Navy? See the World? What the hell are you going on about? You don't know me.

(PHIPPS *re-enters.*)

PHIPPS: Hey you.

(FOGARTY *is a bit startled, but it's directed to* KEVIN.)

PHIPPS: That men's room's a disgrace. When's the last time you ventured in there?

KEVIN: About an hour and a half ago.

PHIPPS: Somebody vomited. It stinks to high heaven.

KEVIN: I know. I cleaned it up already. I sprayed deodorant, but see the problem is, you've got no windows in there, just this pathetic little Fart Fan—

PHIPPS: "Fart Fan." Yes, a lovely piece of graffiti, that. Scrub that off that wall.

(KEVIN *stares at him.*)

PHIPPS: What are you looking at? Are you being insolent? (*Glancing at his shirt pocket*) "Kevin"?

KEVIN: Just making sure you're finished.

PHIPPS: (*Taking out a pad and pencil*) What's your last name, my fine young lad?

KEVIN: O'Rourke. Do you need a spelling?

PHIPPS: (*To* FOGARTY) This is Paul O'Rourke's kid?

(FOGARTY *nods, looking pained by the confrontation.*)

PHIPPS: That explains a lot. (*Back to* KEVIN) Look, I don't care whose kid you are, jack up the quality of the work around here. Start by waxing these floors.

KEVIN: You're not my supervisor.

PHIPPS: Ah, "the child is the father to the man."
How come you didn't join your dad out in Berkeley?
Out there with all the other Free Speechers, huh?

(KEVIN *tries to curtail this by exiting. Before he can:)*

PHIPPS: It's a good thing he left when he did.

KEVIN: What?

PHIPPS: Keep that attitude, young Mr Kevin. Forty years
from now you'll still be modeling the same shirt you're
wearing today.

(PHIPPS *exits.* KEVIN *tries to make eye contact with*
FOGARTY, *to no avail.)*

KEVIN: That was you that threw up in there, wasn't it?

(FOGARTY *exits as* KEVIN *stares after. Scene)*

Scene Three
Kevin's Apartment

(Lights X-Fade to KEVIN'*s Apartment. Sparsely-furnished.
Cheap sofa, floor lamp, end table with small black and white
T V on it. A door U R to street; exit to unseen kitchen and
bedroom D R. Maybe a record playing a torch song, possibly
"My Man."* DARLA *enters wearing a dressing robe long
enough to conceal the fancy dress she has on under it.
She is beautiful and cheerful and goal-directed She busies
herself briefly making sure the apartment is clean and neat,
then exits D R.)*

(KEVIN *enters U R, wearing his work clothes.)*

KEVIN: Darla?

DARLA: Is that my handsome honey?

(KEVIN *flops on couch, tries to decipher something he's
scribbled on a piece of paper)*

KEVIN: Darla, can't you call first? I told you I was busy tonight.

(If record is used, kill music here.)

DARLA: Shut your eyes. I've got something to show you. *(Beat)* Are they shut?

KEVIN: Yeah, they're shut.

(DARLA *enters, having shed the dressing robe to reveal a form-fitting cocktail dress.)*

DARLA: Open.

(KEVIN *takes it in.)*

DARLA: Cat got your tongue, big boy?

KEVIN: Where you going in that, Darla?

DARLA: To meet my Destiny. This is what I'll be wearing next week when they crown me Miss Wakarusa Valley.

KEVIN: You shouldn't get your hopes up.

DARLA: Well, just rain on my parade, Mister Grump Head. *(Beat)* Can't you just say you like it?

KEVIN: You look good in everything, Darla.

DARLA: Ooo, you sweet thing...

(She hugs him. He groans, fends her off)

DARLA: What's the matter?

KEVIN: My neck hurts.

DARLA: How'd you do that?

KEVIN: Some clown rear-ended me.

DARLA: No! They hurt you?

KEVIN: Didn't notice it till now. I was too pissed off.

DARLA: We should get you to the doctor, Kevin.

KEVIN: *(Crossing to wall phone)* I'll be O K Gotta get
through to the insurance guy. *(Dialing)* What's got
me worried, I don't think the sonofabitch was insured.
He never did show me papers. Wouldn': wait for the
cops—hello? Mr Robertson? Hello? Is th:s State Farm?
Can you speak up please? *(Hangs up emphatically)*
It's like he's on the other side of the Moon! Ah,
what a fucked up day.

DARLA: Kevin, you know I don't like Sailor Talk.

KEVIN: *(Beat)* Darla. Please go home.

DARLA: Be nice, can't you?

KEVIN: See, I don't think I can. I'm having such a rotten
day—

DARLA: Rotten days are the days you need me most.

KEVIN: You cooking something? What's :hat smell?

DARLA: Three guesses, first two don't count.

KEVIN: Lasagna?

DARLA: With lots of garlic, just the way you love it.
(Tries to hug him again)

KEVIN: Ah! Careful.

DARLA: Oh, I'm sorry, baby. Here, lie down. *(She helps
as best she can.)* Please let me call a doctor? This could be
serious.

KEVIN: The phone's all screwed up.

DARLA: It was working fine when the plumber used it.

KEVIN: What plumber? When?

DARLA: This afternoon. He fixed your sink, then he
called in to find out where his next job was. You comfy,
hon? Here, let me get you a glass of Chianti.

KEVIN: What was wrong with the sink?

DARLA: *(As she exits to O S kitchen)* Well, I guess it was stopped up or something. I don't know, it's your sink.

KEVIN: Did he leave a bill?

DARLA: *(Off-stage)* He's sending it to your landlady. You want some cheese and crackers?

KEVIN: Naw, don't bother.

DARLA: *(O S)* Be about half an hour more on the pasta. *(She re-enters carrying two glasses of wine.)* You wanna soak in the tub till dinner?

KEVIN: Maybe later.

DARLA: Goodie. We'll do a double-dip, save on the water bill. *(Hands him the wine)*

KEVIN: Thanks, Darla.

DARLA: Starting to feel better, Kevie?

KEVIN: Getting there.

DARLA: Oh, you know that show you like? The one with the creepy little guy who always looks like he's grinding his teeth?

KEVIN: Rod Serling?

DARLA: Yeah, that Twilight Zone thing. It's back on the air. *(Hands him a* T V Guide*)* I never got that show.

KEVIN: *(Reading)* "In His Image." "A man returns to his home to find it taken over by complete strangers." *(He smiles)*

DARLA: You see? I mean, *pardonnez-moi francais*, but what kind of do-do is that? And you know what else hacks me off? The way they make you choose between the last half of Perry Mason and the first half of Dr Kildare. Wouldn't you think that could be avoided?

KEVIN: Well. *(Raises his glass to her)* To a better day tomorrow.

DARLA: And to love! To us. (*She leans over and very carefully kisses him.*) Oh Kevin, I just love my new dress, don't you? (*Quite professionally modeling it*) Is that wrong, Kevin? To love the way you look? Is that a sin or something?

KEVIN: Maybe a venial one.

(*To her doubtful look*)

KEVIN: Itty-bitty.

DARLA: Rudy says this style makes me look like Natalie Wood.

KEVIN: Who's Rudy again?

DARLA: Kevin! My Pageant Coach!

KEVIN: Oh yeah. Tinkerbell.

DARLA: Don't be mean.

(KEVIN *starts to get up*)

DARLA: Where you going?

KEVIN: I gotta try that agent again.

DARLA: (*Gently restraining him*) Tomorrow.

KEVIN: Left rear fender's practically knocked into the tire.

DARLA: You gotta learn to relax. (*She helps him lie back*) Before you go bald or something.

KEVIN: At least I had sense enough to get the creep's license. (*Trying to read his scrap of paper*) "G-S"...something or other.

DARLA: Some people just shouldn't be allowed to drive. Oh! Big news. You know how I was going to do the Shakespeare monologue for my talent? The Lady Macbeth "Unsex me now" thing? It's out. (*She mimes washing blood off her hands.*) "Out, out damn monologue!" This morning Rudy just stared at me, like a sculptor studying a block of granite. "You're not Lady Macbeth," he says. "No. You're a chanteuse. Your soul is French."

KEVIN: *(Struggles to sit up again)* Maybe I will go soak in the tub.

DARLA: *(Restraining him)* Then he asked what my favorite torch song was and it was like, I don't know, a voice from Heaven. I just started singing— *(She does, briefly.)* "Oh my man, I love him so, he'll never know..." *(She has a good voice.)* You know that one? "My Man"?

KEVIN: Uh...

DARLA: No? Oh. Well. Why would you? *(Beat)* The plumber loved my voice. He heard me practicing from back in the bedroom. He said I sounded like a pro. Isn't that sweet?

KEVIN: Yeah, these plumbers, they're real silver-tongued devils, aren't they?

DARLA: Uh-oh. I see a little Glow-worm. Now he's turning greeen...

KEVIN: Sometimes you're just a little too friendly with complete strangers.

DARLA: Well that's just it, he wasn't a complete stranger. He knew all about you.

KEVIN: Really. *(Beat)* What was his name?

DARLA: Kevin. I don't ask strange men their names. I know you think I'm brazen sometimes, but really. I mean, we're practically engaged.

KEVIN: So what did he know about me?

DARLA: He was just real friendly. Wanted to know if we were getting married, and I just said, "Que sera, sera, whatever will be, will be—"

KEVIN: What else?

DARLA: Well, let's see...He knew you were a double major in History and English.

KEVIN: *(Astonished)* He did? The plumber knew that?

DARLA: Yeah, I thought that was kinda weird, too, but he said he knew you from South High, so—

KEVIN: South High.

DARLA: Yeah. And he knew all about your dad. Asked how he was liking Berkeley, were you planning on joining him out there after graduation, and of course I just looked at him and said, "Why would he go out there when I'm right here?"

KEVIN: What did this guy look like?

DARLA: Um...sorta lumpy? Like maybe he had a lot of muscles under his work clothes. Not that I was looking that hard. Kevin? You're not getting jealous, are you? For real?

KEVIN: Darla. Don't talk about me to strangers.

DARLA: But that's what I'm saying. He said he went to South with you.

KEVIN: I went to Saint Xavier.

DARLA: Uh-oh. *(Beat)* I'm sorry, Kevin. I'm just a friendly person.

KEVIN: *(Stares at her thoughtfully)* You know a grad student named Fred Fogarty? Older guy?

DARLA: No...no, I don't think so. Kevin, is there something wrong?

(The phone rings, startling both of them.)

DARLA: Let me. *(She gets it)* Hello?

(Lights up tight X-stage on CLYDE*)*

CLYDE: Darla? Clyde.

DARLA: Hi.

CLYDE: Kevin around?

DARLA: Just a minute. *(To* KEVIN*)* Clyde.

(KEVIN *moves a bit stiffly to the phone.)*

KEVIN: What's up?

CLYDE: Can you hear me O K? You sound far away.

KEVIN: You too. Phone trouble. Speak up.

CLYDE: I'm at the newspaper office, Kev. We've got the police scanner on.

KEVIN: Yeah?

CLYDE: It's Joanna Brady, Kev. She swallowed something. She's at Memorial. That's all I know. *(Silence)* Kev? You there?

KEVIN: Yeah.

CLYDE: You O K?

KEVIN: Is she?

CLYDE: I don't know, Kev. I hope so.

KEVIN: O.K., I'm gone.

CLYDE: Meet you there?

KEVIN: Up to you.

(KEVIN *hangs up. Lights out on* CLYDE.*)*

DARLA: Kevin?

KEVIN: A friend of mine. She's—I've got to go.

DARLA: *(As he exits)* Kevin!

(Scene)

Scene Four
Emergency Room

(Lighting sequence 1: Lights isolate a bed with a sheet or a screen obscuring JOANNA. *2: Spot or isolate another part of the stage on* KEVIN. *He's standing, waiting for permission to see* JOANNA. *After a moment, he glances both ways to make sure he's alone. Then he quickly makes a 'sign of the cross' and inconspicuously says a brief silent prayer. 3: Out of* KEVIN's *sightlines spot or isolate on* CLYDE. *He sees and understands what* KEVIN's *doing and exits before* KEVIN *knows he's there. Out on* CLYDE's *area. 4: Enter* NURSE *into* KEVIN's *area.)*

NURSE: She's awake now. But keep it brief.

*(*KEVIN *crosses with* NURSE *to bedside.)*

NURSE: Joanna, you have a visitor, honey.

*(*NURSE *rearranges the curtain or screen to reveal* JOANNA. *Tubes. Arm to I V, etc. Enough to be a disturbing sight to* KEVIN.*)*

NURSE: It's your brother Kevin.

JOANNA: *(Confused, out of it)* My brother?

(She sees KEVIN *who unobtrusively puts a finger to his lips: say nothing)*

NURSE: I told him he couldn't stay but a short time. *(She exits.)*

JOANNA: *(A small smile)* My brother Kevin...

KEVIN: I knew they'd say "Immediate family only." So I immediately became your family.

(She takes his hand. Pause)

KEVIN: Are you hurting?

JOANNA: *(lets go his hand, points to her throat)* Throat.

KEVIN: They pumped your stomach. *(Wishes he hadn't said it)*

JOANNA: *(Smiles)* I know.

KEVIN: I'm sorry. I...

JOANNA: I'm glad you're here. *(Silence)* Don't try to figure it out.

KEVIN: Does he hurt you?

(JOANNA shakes her head "no")

KEVIN: Well what then? Something's hurting you, Joanna. Just tell me what. I'll make it stop.

JOANNA: It's not working for me.

KEVIN: What?

JOANNA: My life.

KEVIN: *(Beat)* Maybe if you'd let me back into it...

(JOANNA turns away. A beat or two and NURSE re-enters.)

NURSE: Joanna, you have another visitor. It's your husband.

JOANNA: Oh God...

NURSE: That's fine, I'll just tell him you need your rest. *(To KEVIN)* And I'm not making that up either, brother.

KEVIN: Of course, thank you. But it might make some sense to get rid of him first, if you catch my drift.

NURSE: *(Knowingly)* Ah. A little in-law situation here? That's a shame. I'll take care of it.

(NURSE exits. After a moment KEVIN reaches over and takes JOANNA's hand.)

JOANNA: *(A statement)* You like my hand.

(KEVIN nods "yes")

JOANNA: Let it go.

KEVIN: I can't. *(Beat)* I need to know why you do this. Help me. Please.

JOANNA: I'll whisper it.

(KEVIN *leans down. She whispers something. He pulls back, unsettled, perhaps confused.* NURSE *re-enters.)*

NURSE: *(To* KEVIN*)* Coast is clear.

(KEVIN *leans over, kisses her brow, exits. As the* NURSE *pulls the curtain or screen back in place in front of* JOANNA...*)*

NURSE: Things get complicated, don't they, honey?

(Scene)

Scene Five
The Pier, Bluebell Lake #2

(It is just beginning to get light out. Light to full by end of scene.)

(Enter or reveal CLYDE *and* KEVIN, *the latter stretched out flat on pier and* CLYDE *with his feet over the edge. Hold for about five.)*

CLYDE: Your left taillight is out.

KEVIN: I know. Couple guys rear-ended me yesterday.

CLYDE: Um. *(Beat)* You had yourself quite a day.

KEVIN: And here comes another one.

CLYDE: Right on schedule.

KEVIN: *(Beat)* You ever try to kill yourself, Clyde.

CLYDE: Me? Naw, too much trouble. You?

KEVIN: I thought about it once. Back when I was a senior at Saint Xavier. The night Joanna told me she was dumping me.

CLYDE: For Richardson?

KEVIN: Yeah. *(Beat)* Dumped me for a jock. A guy too dumb for lace-up shoes. *(Beat)* I'd kill him if I could get away with it.

CLYDE: He's not that bad a guy, Kev.

KEVIN: He's why she's hooked up to tubes right now!

CLYDE: Is that what she told you?

KEVIN: She didn't have to tell me. It was a stupid goddamn marriage from day one.

CLYDE: Well, yeah, but...what was she supposed to do, Kev?

KEVIN: I don't know! Go visit a sick aunt for a few months. Put it up for adoption. Whatever girls do.

CLYDE: Um. Sure glad I'm not one...bleeding every month.

KEVIN: At least they don't get drafted.

CLYDE: Well, there's that, yeah. *(Beat)* Tyler's thinking about signing up.

KEVIN: He's an idiot.

CLYDE: You don't like anybody much right now, do you?

(KEVIN *doesn't dispute this; may even be a bit chagrined by it.)*

CLYDE: She say anything? When you were in there?

KEVIN: Yeah. *(Beat)* She said she wants to go to Heaven.

CLYDE: She said that?

KEVIN: Whispered it. Like she was saying 'I love you.'

CLYDE: I didn't realize she was so religious.

KEVIN: She's not. This is something...private.
Very specific. Like Oz or Never-Never Land.

CLYDE: *(Beat)* You believe in Heaven?

KEVIN: No. Just Hell.

CLYDE: I saw you praying.

KEVIN: Yeah? Well. Thanks for embarrassing me.
(Beat) Hospitals make people behave funny.

CLYDE: I'm a Mennonite.

KEVIN: What?

CLYDE: I'm a Mennonite.

KEVIN: You're shitting me.

CLYDE: My mother's a Mennonite.

KEVIN: Your father too?

CLYDE: No. He's a businessman.

KEVIN: Don't you have to wear a beard or bib overalls?

CLYDE: That's Amish. Mennonites are way different.
We like cars.

KEVIN: Wow...you think you know someone... *(Beat)*
People are bottomless pits. *(Beat)* I used to be so damn
smart back in high school.

CLYDE: Weren't we all?

KEVIN: *(Pause)* You looking forward to what's next,
Clyde?

CLYDE: What do you mean?

KEVIN: Your life.

CLYDE: Oh, yeah. Tonight my mom's fixing spare ribs.
Then after dinner I'm grabbing my twenty-two, go out
to the dump, shoot a few rats. Wanna come?

(KEVIN *smiles*)

CLYDE: Can't be getting ahead of yourself, Kevin.

KEVIN: *(Beat)* There's this guy at work. He's getting me all messed up. Asking about my plans and all that.

CLYDE: What, he's queer for you?

KEVIN: Don't think the thought hasn't crossed my mind. He even followed me out to the parking lot after my shift, yakking all the way. I thought he was gonna hop in.

CLYDE: Well. Your high school drama teacher found you quite fetching.

KEVIN: Shut up about that.

CLYDE: Sorry.

KEVIN: What is there about me? I draw them like flies. Anyway, I don't think this guy is one of them. He claims he used to be a pilot.

CLYDE: That's a new one.

KEVIN: You think it's a pick-up line?

CLYDE: Did he ask you over to his apartment to show you his uniform?

KEVIN: Navy pilot. Jets. Choppers. Stuff like that. You wouldn't know it to look at him.

CLYDE: He's working Maintenance?

KEVIN: Grad student. G I Bill. He took some courses from my dad.

CLYDE: What's he want with you? Other than maybe your body?

KEVIN: That's the thing. I feel like he's setting me up for something. *(Beat)* To tell you the truth, Clyde, I find him sort of interesting.

CLYDE: *(Mock appalled)* Oh, how efficiently they recruit...

KEVIN: Claims he got shot down. Wounded. Can't fly anymore, so they stuck him in grad school.

CLYDE: Nobody's getting shot down anyplace.

KEVIN: Tell that to Francis Gary Powers.

CLYDE: A fluke. The Russians got lucky with a U-2. He's not flying those, is he?

KEVIN: I think he used to.

CLYDE: You're kidding. Where'd he go down? Cuba?

KEVIN: No, someplace I never heard of. Indochina, I'm thinking. One of those countries over there.

CLYDE: Viet Nam?

KEVIN: Something like that.

CLYDE: I don't think we've got pilots in there, Kev. Just a bunch of mechanics. Supply guys, you know? Advisor-types.

KEVIN: Give me another country.

CLYDE: Uh, Thailand?

(KEVIN *negates it.*)

CLYDE Burma? Cambodia? Jeez. Uh, Laos?

KEVIN: That's it. What you said.

CLYDE: He got shot down in Laos? When?

KEVIN: Couple years ago? Sixty-one?

(CLYDE *stares at him.*)

KEVIN: What?

CLYDE: Don't loan this guy any money.

KEVIN: What, it's a con?

CLYDE: The guy's bullshitting you for some reason or other, Kev. There's nothing going on in Laos.

KEVIN: You're sure?

CLYDE: May I remind you that you're talking to the editor of the Wheatland Daily Student?

KEVIN: According to this guy we've been in a shooting war with the Commies over there since 1960.

CLYDE: Let me explain something to you. Every day I have to read everything that comes off the wires of A P, U P I, Reuters, and Scripps-Howard. Then I decide what we'll print. That's my job. I'm very good at it. Who was the guy they picked as Current Events specialist for Wheatland U in this year's College Bowl Quiz competition? Who?

KEVIN: You were, o revered one.

CLYDE: I was, Kevin, yes, and we beat the hell out of four other schools thanks mostly to me. So stop insulting me here.

KEVIN: Jeez, Clyde, don't have a hernia.

CLYDE: We all have our points of pride, Kevin. If there was a story in Laos, somebody would have broke it.

KEVIN: Air America.

CLYDE: What?

KEVIN: I just remembered. That's who he said he was working for over there. It wasn't the Navy. It was this civilian company. Air America.

CLYDE: Ah-hah...so, what are you saying? We've got American civilians bombing Communist Laotians?

KEVIN: O K! Maybe I've got this wrong. I'm wiped out.

CLYDE: Yeah. Long night. Wanna go to the Holiday Inn, grab some breakfast?

KEVIN: I gotta go to work. Push my broom around, sift butts.

CLYDE: Darla's probably got the State Troopers out looking for you.

KEVIN: Darla. My beauty queen. Clyde, what am I gonna do with her?

CLYDE: She spends more time in your apartment than you do.

KEVIN: It's like dating flypaper. *(Beat)* She makes a helluva lasagna.

CLYDE: Not to be scorned.

(They gather themselves and wearily prepare to exit the pier.)

KEVIN: It's very disturbing, Clyde. This man I hardly know, feeding me all these elaborate lies. Why? Why would he be doing that?

CLYDE: Making up war stories? Kevin, the answers are dark and dreary. Just watch yourself.

(Scene)

Scene Six
Alcove, Wheatland U #2

(FOGARTY is in his place, sitting on the ledge by the fake plants. He's scribbling away on a yellow legal pad. He's intense, as if under deadline pressure. KEVIN enters, pulling a wheeled mop-in-bucket device. He almost turns around when he spies Fogarty, but it's too late.)

FOGARTY: Top o' the morning, Mr O'Rourke.

(KEVIN nods coldly, sets about his cleaning routine)

FOGARTY: Get the number of that guy that whacked you?

(KEVIN *stares at him*)

FOGARTY: Saw you pulling into the parking lot.
Hope your insurance is paid up.

(FOGARTY *laughs briefly and* KEVIN *glowers.*)

FOGARTY: Sorry. No laughing matter. Inappropriate.
I have a condition.

KEVIN: What?

FOGARTY: Pardon?

KEVIN: What's your condition?

FOGARTY: Oh, you don't want to hear about that.

KEVIN: Is it sexual?

FOGARTY: Sorry, did you say "sexual"?

KEVIN: I like girls, Mr Fogarty. You know that,
don't you?

FOGARTY: Oh yeah, you and Darla.

KEVIN: You know about Darla?

FOGARTY: Word on the street is you're engaged.
True? If so, you know: Congratulations. Consequences,
of course. Ramifications, like all choices.

KEVIN: Go on.

FOGARTY: Frankly, it makes you somewhat less
interesting.

KEVIN: Does it?

FOGARTY: In terms of mobility rating, yes, I'm afraid so.
Right now, being single, parentally emancipated and so
on you're pretty close to a four point zero. Pick you up,
move you anywhere on short notice, nobody makes a
fuss. Hook up with Darla, big drop. Maybe down to a
two point eight, thereabouts. It's worth thinking about.

KEVIN: Listen. Leave me alone. Understand? I don't have sex with men.

FOGARTY: *(Bewildered)* I'm aware of that.

KEVIN: Then why are you hitting on me?

FOGARTY: Hitting on you?

KEVIN: Talking about how interesting I am! Talking about picking me up!

FOGARTY: *(Getting it)* You think I'm gay?

KEVIN: *(No clue)* "Gay"? I'm saying you're a homosexual.

(FOGARTY *is amused)*

KEVIN: I'm sorry, but that's how you're coming across. And if that's how it is, well, good for you, but I'm not in the market.

FOGARTY: You're reading this all wrong.

KEVIN: Here's the deal. I don't believe half the stuff you tell me, and I don't feel good about that.

FOGARTY: Which half? Don't you believe?

KEVIN: You don't look like a pilot to me.

FOGARTY: How do they look?

KEVIN: Healthier.

FOGARTY: I used to be very healthy. Before the crash.

KEVIN: Yeah, "the crash," well—in what was it?

FOGARTY: A chopper, Kevin. A UH-34A leased to Air America.

KEVIN: Right, well I've got a friend who should know, and he says he never heard of them, this Air America bunch.

FOGARTY: They don't advertise, Kevin. At least not in the Wheatland Daily Student, as fine a paper as that is.

KEVIN: There's nothing going on in Laos. I looked into it.

(FOGARTY *smiles*)

KEVIN: So you see my problem here. I've got an old guy being too friendly, making up stuff that isn't true, grilling me about my girlfriend, my father, my plans—

FOGARTY: How is your dad, by the way?

KEVIN: See? That bothers me.

FOGARTY: Oh, you're way too sensitive. Your dad was like a mentor to me. I love the man.

KEVIN: Why don't you just transfer, you miss him so much?

FOGARTY: Not that easy. I'm too close to a degree.

KEVIN: They ran him out of town. You know that. Called him names.

FOGARTY: Yes, I know.

KEVIN: "Bad influence on the youth of our state... subversive...disloyal." (*Beat*) Did you speak up for him, Mr Fogarty?

FOGARTY: I made my feelings known. Privately.

KEVIN: Ah, there's the problem. All those other people were making their feelings known publicly. In newspapers. Puts a strain on a marriage.

FOGARTY: Yes, I...I heard about the, uh...

KEVIN: Divorce? Yeah. That sold a few papers, too, didn't it?

FOGARTY: Kevin, it's not so much what a man says. It's where he says it, and when, and to whom.

Disarmament's a tough sell, especially around here. You got Boeing down in Wichita, couple of Air Force bases...your dad stepped in a hornet's nest.

KEVIN: Well. It's a good thing he left when he did, isn't it, Mr Fogarty? Isn't that what your man Phipps said?

FOGARTY: *(looking away, discomforted)* Woe betide well-doers, Kevin.

(Enter DARLA.)

DARLA: There you are! Where were you? Who were you with?

KEVIN: Hey, take it easy.

DARLA: You never called me. I've been up all night, calling the cops, checking hospitals—

KEVIN: You called the cops? C'mere, come over here. *(Leads her as far away from Fogarty as he can)* You gotta settle down, you hear? You're embarrassing me.

DARLA: Embarrassing you? You humiliate me.

KEVIN: This is my workplace. You wanna cost me my job?

DARLA: You're a friggin janitor.

KEVIN: You knew where I was—at Memorial, looking in on a sick friend.

DARLA: Yeah, an old girlfriend. And you weren't there when I showed up.

KEVIN: Right, I was at Bluebell Lake with Clyde, just talking things out, O K? Now will you get a grip?

(PHIPPS enters. FOGARTY seals up the papers he's been working on and engages PHIPPS in a brief [unheard] conversation.)

DARLA: *(A little sigh)* Sometimes I think I just love you too much.

KEVIN: Um. I've gotta get back to work before this guy crawls up my ass.

DARLA: *(Glancing over)* Who, Frog?

KEVIN: You know Fogarty? I asked you before, and you—

DARLA: His name's Fogarty? We always called him Frog. *(Confidingly)* On account of he's so creepy. He asked me for a date once. Can you imagine?

(FOGARTY hands PHIPPS the large envelope, and PHIPPS exits. FOGARTY smiles shyly over at DARLA; she gives him a quick little wave. Then, to KEVIN)

DARLA: Did you really love her, Kevie? That girl in the hospital?

KEVIN: We went to high school. We were neighbors. She's having a tough time.

DARLA: Do you love me?

KEVIN: Hey. What do you think?

DARLA: You shouldn't make me have to ask. *(Gives him a quick kiss)* Chicken parmigiana tonight. Don't be late.

(DARLA exits. KEVIN glances over at FOGARTY who is smiling empathetically.)

FOGARTY: A woman is a full-time job, Kevin.

KEVIN: How do you know Darla?

FOGARTY: We had a class together, briefly. *(Pause)* May I say something personal?

KEVIN: You usually do.

FOGARTY: She's not good for you.

KEVIN: Oh, you think not? *(Smiles)* You'd trade places with me quickly enough.

FOGARTY: How shall I put this? You're one fertilization away from throwing the rest of your life down the toilet. *(Beat)* You're on the cusp, Kevin. The next six months may be the most important in your life. That's gotta be nerve-wracking.

KEVIN: *(Beat)* Who are you?

FOGARTY: Ah, Kevin...the simplest questions are the hardest to answer.

KEVIN: O K, let me try again. What are you?

FOGARTY: In the course of a man's life, he plays many roles. Shakespeare. Right?

KEVIN: What role are you playing right now?

FOGARTY: Well. I guess you could say.... Interviewer.

KEVIN: Uh-huh. So, you're not really a graduate student.

FOGARTY: Oh, indeed I am.

KEVIN: And you really were a pilot?

FOGARTY: Were. Am. Will be. *(Beat)* I'll tell you what I really am. From your perspective? I'm your Fairy Godfather.

*(*KEVIN *reacts)*

FOGARTY: O K, probably an ill-advised word choice. Let me re-phrase it: My job is to help you succeed in what you most want to do.

KEVIN: Uh-huh. And of course you know what that is?

FOGARTY: You want to be heard. *(Beat)* Not easy. Billions of people on the planet, all gobbling away like a bunch of turkeys. All thinking they're saying something. All demanding to be heard. *(Smiles)* Gobble gobble. It's noisy. We drown each other out. We can fix that, Kevin. We can get you published.

KEVIN: So your company, it's a publisher?

FOGARTY: More like a foot in the door. It's all about contacts, Kevin. You're a big boy. You know how that works.

KEVIN: Not what you know, it's who you know?

FOGARTY: First it's who, then it's what. You've got the goods, Kevin. We'll get you jump-started. Newspaper pieces, magazine articles, that sort of thing. Enough to make a plausible living off your writing, maybe generate a little name recognition. You'll take it from there. *(Beat)* Is this starting to sound good to you?

KEVIN: It sounds nuts to me.

FOGARTY: *(Undeterred)* You like poetry, Kevin. Remember the one that goes,
"Full many a rose is born to blush unseen,
And waste its fragrance on the desert air"?

KEVIN: It's "flower," not rose. And "sweetness," not fragrance.

FOGARTY: You're kidding? I've had it wrong all these years? Well, is my face red. Point is, Kevin, we can get you out of this desert. We could put you in a little flat in Greenwich Village—modest, but right where all the action is.

KEVIN: Answer me straight: Are you with the F B I?

FOGARTY: Please don't insult me. *(Beat)* Where were you last October 24th, Kevin?

KEVIN: Here.

FOGARTY: With your dad. Right. Both of you were four minutes away from being vaporized by a Russian SS5 Sandahl missile.

KEVIN: Cuba.

FOGARTY: You know how we can be sure of this, Kevin? Because I took pictures of them. From a U-2 fifteen miles above that island. *(Smiles)* It gives one a unique perspective.

KEVIN: You make me nervous, Mr Fogarty.

FOGARTY: How so?

KEVIN: You sound like a man who's spent way too much time watching James Bond movies. I mean, U-2s, combat missions...I watch you pee your pants every time Phipps walks by.

FOGARTY: Forget about me! I'm nothing. I. Don't. Matter. What matters is this, Kevin. We're at war. We could lose. Easily. If we lose, civilization loses.

KEVIN: What are you going on about? Viet Nam? Kennedy's not stupid enough to get us caught up in that.

FOGARTY: Eight months ago your beloved Kennedy had his finger on a red button that could blow the world to smithereens. So did the imbecilic son of a coal miner over in Russia. *(Beat)* Get your head out of your ass, young man. You're living your life in ignorance. Right now, clear over on the other side of this bucolic little world you're so blissfully inhabiting, there are thousands of little yellow people wearing black pajamas, and they want to kill you.

KEVIN: Look, I'm very confused by you. Are you in the military? What is this company you're working for?

FOGARTY: I'm working for the United States of America, Kevin. Aren't we all?

KEVIN: This is surreal.

FOGARTY: My world is painfully real.

KEVIN: Fred—may I call you Fred? Why me? Of all people?

FOGARTY: You're the father's son.

KEVIN: I don't know what that means.

FOGARTY: You're a thinker. Potentially an opinion-maker.

KEVIN: No, let me tell you what I am. I'm a twenty year old double major in history and English. The second I set foot off a college campus, I'll get re-classified and drafted.

FOGARTY: And you'd proudly go, wouldn't you? *(Silence)* Well. Politics is remediable. *(Beat)* As for the deferment, no worries. We'll start you at GS7 or 8. Untouchable. Instantly, and for the duration.

KEVIN: Uh-huh. Can we go back a bit? Sorry if you've filled me in on this already. My processing seems impaired. What is it you want me to do for you?

FOGARTY: We want you to help us stem the tides of history.

KEVIN: Ah.

FOGARTY: Our goal is to do that silently, under cover of darkness. America is asleep, and that's fine. We don't want to disturb her. We merely want to save her.

(KEVIN *is studying* FOGARTY *very intently, and* FOGARTY *calmly returns the stare.)*

KEVIN: What's your position on Free Will, Mr Fogarty?

FOGARTY: I'm in favor of it when it's not inconvenient.

KEVIN: O K. I'm going to will myself not to believe one word you've said to me. Not one. What do you say to that?

FOGARTY: First you think I'm gay. Now you think I'm crazy.

KEVIN: Prove that you're not.

FOGARTY: That's a tough one. *(Thinks it over)* I predict that something catastrophic will happen before this year's out.

KEVIN: That's a safe bet. Can't you tell me something I don't know?

FOGARTY: You sure you want me to?

(KEVIN nods—a bit apprehensively?)

FOGARTY: Your friend? The Joanna Brady girl?

KEVIN: You know about her?

FOGARTY: Her parents are going to institutionalize her in the Psych Ward at Topeka State Hospital.

(KEVIN is speechless. PHIPPS enters.)

PHIPPS: Mr Fogarty.

FOGARTY: Sir?

PHIPPS: A word with you, please.

(FOGARTY starts to exit, turns back to KEVIN.)

FOGARTY: I'm sorry. I couldn't think of anything else.

(FOGARTY exits.)

(Scene)

Scene Seven
Kevin's Apartment #2

(A few days later. DARLA is stretched out on KEVIN's couch. She's wearing shorts or "pedal-pusher" slacks. Her legs are straight up in the air. She's reading a newspaper.)

(It's late afternoon, early evening, and she's yelling to KEVIN [who's got a costume change here].)

DARLA: Hey Kevin, I need a favor. Can you hear me?

KEVIN: *(O S)* Yeah.

DARLA: I've got an audition Tuesday afternoon over at Centron Studios. They're shooting some kind of educational film. Like a fake documentary? Anyway, my car's gonna be in the shop.

(KEVIN enters. Decent-looking slacks, polo shirt; maybe carrying a cup of coffee.)

KEVIN: What's wrong with it this time?

DARLA: The hydraulic system? Something like that. Can you give me a lift?

KEVIN: I'll have to check with my Appointments Secretary. *(Takes a section of the newspaper)*

DARLA: Kevin...

KEVIN: How can you read the paper like that?

DARLA: It's yoga. It's a spiritual thing. And it keeps my legs from bloating. *(Glancing over at him)* You look nice, Kevie. I better get a move on or you'll be ashamed to be seen in public with me.

(KEVIN realizes he may have a problem.)

DARLA: What time does it start?

KEVIN: Uh, what, exactly?

DARLA: *(Slightly exasperated)* You know. The Rock Hudson Doris Day movie.

KEVIN: Oh that. Yeah...let me look it up. *(As he pretends to be doing so)* Hey, you know that guy at work? Fogarty?

DARLA: Frog? Yeah?

KEVIN: He says you took a class with him?

DARLA: Yeah, for a couple weeks. Your dad's class. Wow. You wouldn't think a class called "Game Theory" could be so boring.

KEVIN: What was he like? Around my dad.

DARLA: Big brown-noser. Shameless. Took notes the whole class. I mean like a Court Stenographer. Then, after every lecture? Zoom. Up to the front of the room, first in line, grinning his face off like your dad was some big celebrity or something. (*Beat*) He's not, is he?

KEVIN: Did my dad seem to like him?

DARLA: Kevin, I don't know. I only took the stupid class to meet you. Soon as I realized you'd firked out, I was Gone with the Wind. Hey look! Here's an article on the Miss Wakarusa Valley pageant. I wonder if my name's in it? (*She reads the piece with growing horror.*) Oh no. Oh, this is...shit!

KEVIN: (*Mock reprimand*) I hear Sailor Talk...

DARLA: Kevin! They cancelled it! They called it off! (*Thrusts the article at him*)

KEVIN: (*Reading aloud*) "All our Wakarusa belles are beauties and we refuse to discriminate."

DARLA: "Discriminate!"

KEVIN: "...board will bestow this distinction...later date...on a housewife who can cook."

DARLA: "Housewife who can cook!" That's what they want? Why didn't they just run a freaking Want Ad?

KEVIN: Hey baby, you can outcook any of them.

DARLA: That's not the point, Kevin, is it? (*She's close to crying.*) The point is...I'm prettier than them. And now nobody will know it.

KEVIN: I know it. Who else needs to?

DARLA: *(Quietly)* Me.

KEVIN: *(Moves to comfort her)* Aw baby...

DARLA: *(Hugging him)* I don't get to sing "My Man."

KEVIN: Sing it to me.

DARLA: Oh, you hate that stuff. *(Beat)* There was a five hundred dollar scholarship. I coulda used that.

KEVIN: There'll be other contests, Darla. Won't there? Aren't there always?

DARLA: Only Miss Military Ball. And my dress is all wrong for that. *(Beat)* Maybe they'll take it back. Give me a credit? I mean, I never wore it.

KEVIN: I'll bet they will. And I'll tell you something else. I got a good feeling for you on this Centron audition.

DARLA: You do?

KEVIN: It's your time, Darla. You're due.

(DARLA is calming down. She says the following without rancor or malice.)

DARLA: I'll tell you what's really going on with this Wakarusa Valley nonsense. They're afraid Elisha Stryker's gonna sue them.

KEVIN: Sorry, Elisha who?

DARLA: She's a colored girl, and she didn't make it to the finals. Why else are they going on about "we refuse to discriminate," huh?

KEVIN: *(Discomforted)* I think they want us to call them "Negroes," Darla.

DARLA: Oh, who cares? I'm so depressed.

(There's a knock at the door.)

KEVIN: Come on in, Clyde!

DARLA: What's Clyde doing here? I thought we were going to the movies?

(CLYDE *enters.*)

CLYDE: Darla.

DARLA: Hi, Clyde. What brings you here?

CLYDE: Heading over to Topeka State, look in on Joanna Brady.

DARLA: *(To* KEVIN, *accusingly)* You, too?

KEVIN: Yeah, me too.

DARLA: We had a date!

KEVIN: Yeah, I screwed up. *(Beat)* You can come with us if you want.

DARLA: Oh, that's a swell way to spend an evening. Hanging around a nuthouse with your one true love. Well. I won't make a scene. Not in front of your only living friend. *(She grabs her bag and huffs past* CLYDE.*)* You have a real fun night now, Clyde.

CLYDE: Uh...O K.

(DARLA *exits.* CLYDE *looks a bit overwhelmed.* KEVIN *takes it in stride.*)

KEVIN: Hi Clyde.

CLYDE: Well I feel stupid.

KEVIN: Don't worry about. What's that? *(Indicating some envelopes* CLYDE's *been holding)*

CLYDE: Oh. Grabbed your mail on the way in.

(KEVIN *takes it)*

CLYDE: I've never seen her that mad.

KEVIN: She's super-pissed because they cancelled her beauty contest.

CLYDE: Oh yeah. The Wakarusa Valley thing. You know the joke going around? "Cancelled on account of ugliness."

(KEVIN *opens one of the envelopes, shows* CLYDE *the contents.*)

KEVIN: Two hundred bucks.

CLYDE: Your daddy is good to you.

KEVIN: It's not from him. (*Reads from a note enclosed with the cash*) "Fix your fender."

CLYDE: That's it? No signature? No address?

KEVIN: (*Inspecting envelope*) Local postmark.

CLYDE: Man, your insurance agent is psycho.

KEVIN: I know who this is from. My fairy godfather.

CLYDE: Not the Laos guy? Mr True Adventure?

KEVIN: Freddy the Fog.

CLYDE: Whew. That guy wants you bad.

KEVIN: Let me ask you something. Say somebody offered you a job. Right out of school. They take care of your draft deferment. All you have to do is keep doing the one thing you most want to do, and they'll pay you to do it. They help you along and then, right when you're really making it, a government pension kicks in for the rest of your life. You interested?

CLYDE: (*Contemplating him*) You've been summoning up the Devil again, haven't you? (*Beat*) Where do I sign? And does it have to be in blood?

(*Phone rings.*)

KEVIN: Hello? Dad! Listen, I got the Thanksgiving flight booked. I tried calling you on that a couple days ago but they said you been disconnected. They paying you that bad out there? (*Joke over—concern grows as he listens*)

You think? Oh boy...well, what should I do? *(Beat)* Why is this happening, Dad? Do people hate you? *(Beat)* Are you safe? Can you just tell me that?

CLYDE: Ask him about Fogarty.

KEVIN: Oh Dad—you remember a grad student named Fogarty? *(Beat)* You mean that? But Dad, it's like he worships you...O K, yeah. I hear you. Wow. Listen, what if I need to get hold of you, I mean if you're traveling and all? Hello? Dad? *(He hangs up. He seems lost.)*

CLYDE: You O K?

KEVIN: Cut off. Pay phone, I think...

CLYDE: What's he say about Fogarty?

KEVIN: Stay away.

CLYDE: Really?

KEVIN: Just stay away. And he says his phone was tapped.

CLYDE: He's sure?

KEVIN: Says mine may be, too. Wants me to disconnect it.

CLYDE: Darla is not going to like that.

KEVIN: You have to make a joke out of everything? Aren't you alarmed by any of this, Clyde?

CLYDE: Any of what? Nothing's happening to me. *(Beat)* Maybe not to your dad, either.

KEVIN: What's that mean? My dad's paranoid?

CLYDE: He's a professor, isn't he? Sooner or later, they all get that way.

KEVIN: *(Glancing at his watch)* Look, if we're gonna go see Joanna, we gotta get on the road.

CLYDE: Yeah, about this Topeka pilgrimage—

KEVIN: You bailing out on me?

CLYDE: Is she actually expecting us?

KEVIN: I left it sorta open.

CLYDE: Then I got a better idea. Let's go to Fogarty's.

KEVIN: Are you nuts? My dad just told me to stay away from him.

CLYDE: C'mon. You haven't done anything your dad wanted since you were twelve.

KEVIN: What's with this, Clyde? Up till now Fogarty's just been one big queer joke to you.

CLYDE: I find it fascinating that your dad, who fears no one, seems to fear him.

KEVIN: It sounded more like contempt than fear.

CLYDE: Kevin, Fogarty got shot down in Laos. I can't get that out of my head.

KEVIN: But you don't believe that.

CLYDE: I had a nightmare last night. Or maybe it was just an attack of humility. I heard this sarcastic voice saying, Clyde, what if you really don't know everything? What if it's true? What if there's really a secret shooting war in Laos, and you, Clyde, were too arrogant to even check it out?

KEVIN: You'd have to kiss that Pulitzer goodbye, huh?

CLYDE: I woke up in a cold sweat. And what about you, Kevin? Forget foreign affairs. What's Fogarty know about domestic affairs?

KEVIN: Meaning?

CLYDE: What's he know about your dad? Or the divorce? You can beat yourself to death wondering for the rest of your life. Or you could ask Fogarty.

KEVIN: Clyde, I'm telling you, there's something not right about him. I think he's a little nuts.

CLYDE: Kevin. Aren't we all?

KEVIN: Even my dad, huh Clyde?

CLYDE: Maybe not entirely. *(Beat)* Even paranoiacs have enemies.

KEVIN: That plumber tapped my phone, Clyde. I know damn well he did.

CLYDE: Think back to those guys that rear-ended you. Two of them, right? One pushing you around, giving you shit about insurance and all? *(Beat)* What was the other guy doing?

KEVIN: I never noticed.

CLYDE: You're being surveilled, Kevin.

KEVIN: It's feeling that way. But why?

CLYDE: *(like a shrug)* It happens.

KEVIN: Not to us. Not to me. I'm nobody.

CLYDE: Blame your dad. It's him they're after. *(Beat)* You're being used, Kevin. That's all.

(KEVIN *is silent for a space. Then he gets up, pulls on a light jacket, and exits to the street without a word or a look back.* CLYDE *follows him out. Scene)*

Scene Eight
Fogarty's Apartment and a Prison Cell in Moscow

(Isolate initially on a portion of FOGARTY's *apartment. He's stretched out on a recliner; he's in a reverie induced in no small part by his medications.)*

FOGARTY: My dad and me, we used to carve model airplanes. Balsa wood, straight out of Model Airplane News. He'd always say, "Are we done yet?" And I'd say, "No sir, not quite," and I'd carve me up a little man and put him in the cockpit. "That's me," I'd say. "That's me flying." And he'd laugh. *(Beat)* My dad, he had a weird little laugh.

(Lights up dim on cell of U-2 pilot, now prisoner, FRANCIS GARY POWERS. *For* FOGARTY *the time remains Summer 1963, but for* GARY *the time is August 11, 1960. He has just been sentenced to ten years in prison for piloting the spy plane shot down over Sverdlovsk on May 1, 1960. When we first see him,* GARY *is sitting on a cot. When he stands beneath his bare light bulb, we see his drab pajama-like prison garb beneath the thin blanket he's wrapped himself in.)*

(Production Note: It's important that POWERS *be vertically higher than* FOGARTY. *The preference is that* GARY *not interact directly or unambiguously with* FOGARTY.*)*

FOGARTY: Model Airplane News. Now there was a magazine. Those boys knew their stuff. Remember the March 1958 issue?

GARY: *(Stands, recites as if reading)* "An unconfirmed rumor says that U-2s are flying across the Iron Curtain taking aerial photographs."

FOGARTY: Model Airplane News blows our cover! *(Laughs)* Thank God for a free press, huh Powers?

GARY: They weren't supposed to be able to see us.

FOGARTY: Too high for radar! Yeah boy, there's one we all wanted to believe. Too high for radar and no visible contrail.

GARY: Ten years in Ljubyanka Prison.

FOGARTY: Oh Gary, you'll be out in a year and a half. They'll swap you for a German spy, and half the country will scream we got screwed.

GARY: Ten years.

FOGARTY: You just don't know that yet. Every day you'll be doing ten in your mind.

GARY: Dad hears the translation. Stands. Screams at the Judge, "I'd rather be dead than spend ten years in a Russian prison!"

FOGARTY: (*A small laugh*) Be glad he's your dad and not your lawyer.

GARY: He'll talk to Khruschev, he says. One coal miner to another. He'll get me out.

FOGARTY: He will. He does. (*Beat*) You're the son of a good man. Make the old man proud.

GARY: I can do this. This aloneness.

FOGARTY: Yes, we're good at that.

GARY: Can do. Can do.

(*Sound: a doorbell ringing. Lights dim out on* GARY *as he stretches out on his cot. More of* FOGARTY'*s unkempt apartment becomes visible.*)

(FOGARTY *struggles to regain control of his senses. He tries to assess what, if anything, needs to be hidden.*)

FOGARTY: Who is it?

KEVIN: *(O S)* It's Kevin O'Rourke. Can I see you for a second?

FOGARTY: It's kind of a bad time—

KEVIN: *(O S)* It's important.

FOGARTY: *(To himself)* Shit. *(Beat)* Hold on.

(Ideally there's a functional door, and when FOGARTY *opens it, we can see both* KEVIN *and* CLYDE *standing there.)*

FOGARTY: Who's this?

KEVIN: This is my friend Clyde.

CLYDE: Hello, Mr Fogarty.

FOGARTY: You're the Mennonite?

KEVIN: *(Glancing at* CLYDE*)* I must have mentioned....

CLYDE: I'm with the student paper, Mr Fogarty. We're doing a piece on Wheatland students attending on the G I Bill, and Kevin thought you could help me out.

FOGARTY: Look, my place is a mess.

CLYDE: It would mean a lot to me. I've got a grade riding on this, and a deadline.

FOGARTY: How long's this gonna take?

CLYDE: Five minutes max.

*(*FOGARTY *relents, motions for them to enter.)*

FOGARTY: Just kick things off chairs, or...I'm used to moving around a lot, so I never really unpack.

CLYDE: Hey, you should see my place. *(Taking out a pad and pencil)* Let me just get the usual here before we delve further. Where were you born, Mr Fogarty?

FOGARTY: Mansfield, Ohio. Farm near there.

CLYDE: And your age?

FOGARTY: *(Hesitates)* Old.

CLYDE: *(Smiling, genial)* Thirty-five?

FOGARTY: That neighborhood. *(Attempting levity)* Don't want to scare off all the co-eds.

CLYDE: Kevin says you were in the Navy? A pilot? What did you fly?

FOGARTY: When? During Korea?

CLYDE: Korea. Sure.

FOGARTY: Sabres. F-80s, F-84s.

CLYDE: That must have been exciting.

FOGARTY: It was terrifying. I hated every second of it.

CLYDE: Oh.

FOGARTY: We aren't all heroes.

CLYDE: No, I guess not. So you got out after Korea?

FOGARTY: No, I re-upped.

CLYDE: Even though you hated it?

FOGARTY: What I hated was getting shot at by MiG-15s. *(Beat)* The flying. I love the flying.

CLYDE: Uh-huh. So where have you been stationed since then?

FOGARTY: *(Uneasy)* I thought you were going to ask me about the G I Bill?

CLYDE: Kevin mentioned you were in Laos?

FOGARTY: *(Staring at* KEVIN*)* Did he.

CLYDE: Got shot down there or something? Our readers might be interested in that.

FOGARTY: Why?

CLYDE: Because we aren't supposed to be there, Mr Fogarty.

(FOGARTY *reaches over and turns on a radio. Sound:
Unobtrusive instrumental—bland Ferrante and Teicher-
type stuff.)*

FOGARTY: You're about to get in way over your head,
young man.

CLYDE: The Geneva Conference last year neutralized all
factions, so I'm guessing you were there before that?

FOGARTY: It's time for you to go now. Here's a quote
for your story: "I thank God for the G I bill, and I
absolutely love Wheatland University." Goodbye.
And Kevin, call first next time.

KEVIN: My phone's fucked up. *(Beat)* Tell him about
Air America, Fred.

CLYDE: Yes, what exactly is that?

FOGARTY: It's a civilian carrier based in Thailand.
And Kevin, I'm very hurt that you set me up this way.
I don't deserve this.

KEVIN: You know things you shouldn't.

FOGARTY: Do I?

KEVIN: And you know things I should.

FOGARTY: Is this about the Joanna Brady girl? Cause if it
is, the only thing you should be asking is, Was I right?
About the Psych Ward? *(Beat)* Yes. I was. And I'm very
sorry. Life is cruel sometimes.

KEVIN: That's deep, Fred.

CLYDE: How many men do we have in Laos?

FOGARTY: Over. Go.

CLYDE: Can we talk later, Mr Fogarty?

FOGARTY: No.

KEVIN: Do you know who rear-ended me that day?

FOGARTY: Kevin. I no longer know what I know.

KEVIN: *(looking around)* I wanted to thank you for the two hundred bucks you sent, but Fred, this place is a dump. You live worse than I do. *(Beat)* Couldn't have come from you. So. Who do I thank?

FOGARTY: It's past your bedtime, children.

CLYDE: Mr Fogarty, are there spies on this campus, and are you one of them?

FOGARTY: Who do I look like, James Bond? You two have a lot of balls coming into my apartment and fucking interrogating me. *(To* KEVIN*)* And you. What hair crawled up your ass?

KEVIN: I talked to my dad about you today. Or do you already know that?

FOGARTY: Oh, now we get to it.

KEVIN: "Stay away from him. Don't talk to him." That's all he'd say.

FOGARTY: That saddens me.

KEVIN: Why's he say that? Make sense of it for me.

FOGARTY: You ask too much.

KEVIN: There must be a reason, a moment in time. Please try to remember.

FOGARTY: I told you. My memories are contaminated. I can't remember what I'm supposed to know and what I'm not. What happened, what didn't. Who I can say what to. Who I did say what to.

KEVIN: DID YOU HURT MY FATHER? *(Silence)* Are you still hurting him?

FOGARTY: You want "yes" or "no" for everything. But everything is "yes" and "no."

KEVIN: Get out of my life. And stay out of my dad's.

(KEVIN *exits.*)

CLYDE: He'll feel better when he gets his phone fixed. *(Beat, indicating the two of them)* We'll talk.

*(*CLYDE *exits. As* FOGARTY *returns broodingly to his recliner, lights come up briefly on* GARY. FOGARTY *shakes some pills out of couple bottles, swills them down, and stares into space.* GARY *in his prison cell looks like* FOGARTY'*s twin.)*

(Lights fade on both of them to blackout.)

END OF ACT ONE

ACT TWO
ICARUS

Scene Nine
Day Room, Topeka State Hospital

(October 1963. Lights up on a cheap table and two Formica chairs D S. KEVIN is seated, waiting for JOANNA. She appears far U S, sees him before he spots her. The effect is as if we are viewing her at the end of a long corridor. She has been given permission to wear one of her own skirts and blouses for this visit. This is a rescindable privilege based upon a "level" reflecting her compliance with the myriad protocols of the Psych Ward. Her unguarded first look is one of apprehension, but she smiles as she walks D S towards him, and he stands when he spots her. They sit and navigate a moment of silence, of shyness.)

KEVIN: You look especially pretty today.

JOANNA: You give me a reason. *(Beat)* How's Darla?

KEVIN: Oh, still pursuing her dream.

JOANNA: Queen for a Day?

KEVIN: She's a finalist in another one. Miss Military Ball. *(Beat)* Something.

JOANNA: She still making a scene every time you come to see me?

KEVIN: Yeah. On Saturdays, along with the evening performance, she throws in a free matinee.

JOANNA: I'm sorry. For you. For her.

KEVIN: Last Thursday she threw herself in front of a car.

(JOANNA *reacts;* KEVIN'*s dismissive*)

KEVIN: Ahh, it was only going about ten miles an hour. And she made damn sure I saw it.

JOANNA: You tried to break up with her?

(KEVIN *nods*)

JOANNA: I see stuff like that a dozen times a day in here.

KEVIN: You two should switch places.

(*This inspires another moment of silent awkwardness.*)

JOANNA: You seem really depressed, Kevin.

KEVIN: Well. You should know.

JOANNA: Yes. I should. I do.

KEVIN: It's 1963. Everybody's depressed.

JOANNA: *(Smiling)* Not the Beatles.

KEVIN: No. Not the Beatles.

JOANNA: *(Softly)* "She Loves You..."

KEVIN: *(Softly, smiling)* "yeah, yeah, yeah..."

(JOANNA *reaches over and takes* KEVIN'*s hand. A* VOICE— *a nurse's* VOICE—*is heard as if through an intercom, mildly amplified. One must surmise at this point that* JOANNA *and* KEVIN *are being observed by someone off-stage, perhaps from behind a one-way glass. The effect should not be comedic; if it is, it will be necessary to cast an on-stage Orderly to function as a sort of chaperone during this scene.*)

VOICE: (*O S*) No physical contact.

(JOANNA *puts her hands back in her lap.* KEVIN *doesn't react—it's a rule, and he's heard it before.*)

JOANNA: How's your so-called "pilot?" Is he still coming onto you?

KEVIN: No. It was never like that, I don't think. Though with this guy, you never know. You're around him more than thirty seconds, boom, it's like you're Alice falling down the rabbit hole. *(Beat)* He ratted out my dad. Did I tell you?

JOANNA: How do you mean, Kevin?

KEVIN: Things got said. In confidence, in private. They got out. I track it to him.

JOANNA: Are you sure?

KEVIN: No, I'm not sure of anything. Not any more. *(Beat)* What's making me crazy is he claims he loves my dad. Like as a mentor thing, you know? So how do you figure that, Joanna, huh? How does that add up?

JOANNA: I've never been any good at math.

KEVIN: No, me neither.

JOANNA: So this man is dangerous, you think?

KEVIN: He's backed off. *(Beat)* Maybe he's just a little crazy.

JOANNA: Well, he does sound like he satisfies some of our prerequisites.

KEVIN: You think?

JOANNA: Well, he's got his little "story," doesn't he? Fighter pilot war hero?

KEVIN: No, he knows he's not the hero.

JOANNA: Does he claim any special powers or attributes?

KEVIN: Nope. I've never seen a man so attributeless. *(Beat)* What are you saying? You think Fogarty belongs in here?

JOANNA: Oh, I don't know, Kevin. The mind's a labyrinth. But if he's not harmful to you or himself, what does it matter? This percentage of truth, that percentage of fantasy...whatever makes him happy.

KEVIN: He's not. He might be the saddest man I've ever met. *(Beat)* But he doesn't belong in Topeka State Hospital. No more than you do.

JOANNA: No? Then where? Where do I belong?

KEVIN: With me.

JOANNA: Don't start that.

KEVIN: You could be out of here by noon tomorrow. You know how to manipulate these people. Just say what you've got to say.

JOANNA: Don't get intense on me.

KEVIN: You censor me. All the time.

JOANNA: Nothing personal. I censor myself, too.

KEVIN: You invent your pain, and then you fall in love with it.

JOANNA: Is that what I do?

KEVIN: No, I'm sorry.

JOANNA: You may be right. It gets to be a form of art with some of us, the shaping of pain. It's about all we have to play with around here.

KEVIN: Don't you miss your baby?

JOANNA: *(Pause)* Not so much anymore. His grandparents, they're better at it than I was. Look, you've got to go now.

KEVIN: I love you, Joanna.

JOANNA: Stop it. If you want to come back here, just stop it.

(KEVIN *falls silent.*)

JOANNA: You know why I'm here? I'm here to get away from intense people. I'm here to be sedated. I'm here to think about Heaven, way up there above all these clouds, Kevin. Way up there on the seventh level, second mezzanine, row C, seat twelve—the one that's got my name on it. That's where I'm going, Kevin, as fast as I can get there. *(Smiles)* If it's not already taken, I'll save the seat next to me for you.

KEVIN: I've got a better idea. Let me take you out to the high desert. We'll camp. Watch the sun go down over darkening mountains, and the stars, glistening, glistening like tears, whirling over your head like you're drunk. You'll sleep. You'll rest. But you can't tell for sure because all night long you dream of those stars whirling over you. And in your dream you hear yourself asking, "Did I remember to close my eyes? Am I sleeping yet?" *(Beat)* And then this wonderful thing happens. It gets light out. Birds you never see are amazed! They get another day, and they're so grateful, they explode with joy. And you smell the air, and it's Eden, and the flowers want to smell it, too, and they all open up to get a good whiff, and it's perfume, perfume out there. Reds and pinks and yellows, and they don't think, oh Christ, I'm still stuck in this desert! No! No, they say, "I'm alive. I'm alive."

(She reaches over and takes his hand. Immediately, the amplified VOICE *of nurse.)*

VOICE: *(O S)* No physical contact.

(She tries to take her hand away. He won't let her. She is weeping quietly. Exhausted, she lays her head on their hands, resting on the table.)

VOICE: *(O S)* That's a level drop, Joanna.

(She pulls herself together enough to break free and move off U S towards her exit. One look back, then gone.)

(Scene)

Scene Ten
The Library

(Lights up on FOGARTY. *At first he's in an unidentifiable neutral space which soon becomes suggestive of a stack in a library. He's well-dressed—suit, tie—and is holding what turns out to be a Vietnamese dictionary. He's talking to somebody we can't see right away.)*

FOGARTY: First U-2C ever shipped to Japan. Pratt and Whitney J-75. Seventeen thousand pounds of thrust kicking you in the ass.

(Lights up on GARY *at his cot in his cell. He's more participatory than in his last scene with* FOGARTY, *but the preference is that they not make eye contact.)*

(The effect is perhaps that of cellmates or soldiers talking after "lights out." Quiet; trapped.)

GARY: Four years ago now was it? You set the record?

FOGARTY: Two records. Remember?

GARY: Highest U-2 flight ever...

FOGARTY: And lowest.

GARY: *(Smiling)* Ran outta gas. Put her down on a...what was it?

FOGARTY: Japanese Glider Club.

GARY: Right.

FOGARTY: Ten miles south of Atsugi. *(Beat)* Never saw so many photographers. Like a Debutantes Ball. The U-2 coming out party. Boy, were they pissed.

GARY: That was a good landing, though. In the mud like that?

FOGARTY: (*Appreciative*) I thought it was, too, Gary.

(*By this line lights up on* KEVIN. *He's working on a book-strewn desk or carrel—or he was till he became aware of* FOGARTY *and started eavesdropping on his end of the* GARY *conversation.*)

GARY: Saved the plane. Saved yourself. Set the world's altitude record, Fred. Don't be forgetting that part.

FOGARTY: (*Smiling*) Held it for almost a week.

GARY: You've been to the edge of the world. How many men can say that?

(*Lights are dimming on* GARY.)

FOGARTY: High Fliers.

GARY: High Fliers.

(*Lights out on* GARY, *up further on* KEVIN. FOGARTY *is startled to discover him.* KEVIN *makes a small point of glancing around before asking—*)

KEVIN: Am I intruding?

FOGARTY: Sometimes when I'm alone I talk out loud to myself.

KEVIN: (*A bit embarrassed*) Well. That's all right. (*Beat*) Been a while.

FOGARTY: Yes.

KEVIN: You're dressing better these days. Did you come into some money?

FOGARTY: Oh, uh, I'm escorting a guest of the University. Madame Nhu's father? He's speaking at the Auditorium tonight.

KEVIN: Madame Nhu? The Dragon Lady?

FOGARTY: She doesn't like to be called that.

KEVIN: I'll pass the word.

FOGARTY: She was our original speaker. But what with her recent widowing...

KEVIN: Yes. Tragic. What was the guy's name again?

FOGARTY: Ngo Dinh Diem.

KEVIN: Right. General Diem. The guy running South Vietnam. Got his pink slip, did he? Terminated? That what you call it?

FOGARTY: No, Kevin. I call it a war. Now it's on for real.

KEVIN: Well, I'm sure Madame Nhu will land on her feet.

FOGARTY: Why don't you come tonight?

KEVIN: To the Aud? Why? So I can hear a two-hour lecture in broken English on the theme of "Send us more of your money"?

FOGARTY: There's a reception afterwards. I'll add your name to the Guest List.

KEVIN: When did you get to have so much pull?

FOGARTY: I try to be useful. *(Hefting a dictionary)* I speak a bit of Vietnamese, a little French...

KEVIN: A man of many facets. *(Dismissing him)* I've got a major paper due.

(KEVIN returns to his books. FOGARTY continues to stand around. Finally, irritably—)

KEVIN: What?

FOGARTY: I may be going away soon.

KEVIN: Um. Good thing you never unpack.

FOGARTY: There are things you should know.

KEVIN: Spare me any more of your shit about the Company.

FOGARTY: They're no longer interested in you.

KEVIN: Really? Does this mean I can hock my phone up again?

FOGARTY: *(Beat)* I'm sure this is fun for you. But you really don't know enough to judge me.

KEVIN: And I'll be the judge of that, too.

FOGARTY: I didn't set out to betray your father.

KEVIN: Well. Accidents happen.

FOGARTY: *(Beat)* I can help him, if you let me.

KEVIN: I don't trust you as far as I can spit.

FOGARTY: If I can hurt him, I can help him. Stands to reason.

KEVIN: Can you just fuck off? Can you do that for me?

FOGARTY: Your father's in some jeopardy. Which would you rather do, help him or curse me?

KEVIN: *(Still library-quiet but furious)* You took his classes just to inform on him.

FOGARTY: Not true. I took his classes to learn. *(Beat)* But in the interests...of the moment, of...accuracy, I will tell you this. I was required to share my notes.

KEVIN: With?

FOGARTY: Others.

(A pause. KEVIN seems almost relieved to hear this.)

KEVIN: I'm guessing...not Darla?

(FOGARTY smiles a little.)

KEVIN: So what you are, then, is what we technically call "a fucking rat"?

(FOGARTY *is quite hurt by that, perhaps surprisingly so even to himself. He can say nothing for a time.*)

FOGARTY: Everybody gets used by somebody.

KEVIN: Including me by you. To control my dad.

FOGARTY: That's not inconsistent with a benign intent. If a child is running into traffic and you grab it out of harm's way—

KEVIN: *(Decides)* O K. Got the point. You want me to convey a message to him.

FOGARTY: By way of undoing whatever inadvertent ill I've done him.

KEVIN: Sure.

FOGARTY: Tell him the friends he's making at Livermore and White Sands are not reliable. Cut them off.

KEVIN: That it?

FOGARTY: Your father likes games. Apparently there's a kind of computer game called Omega. Sort of about... Vietnam. And no matter how they program the damn thing, it keeps saying we're going to lose.

KEVIN: Maybe it's a Communist computer.

FOGARTY: Your father knows all about this. He's not supposed to, but he does.

KEVIN: It's called Research. That's his job.

FOGARTY: And he's good at it. The problem is, if he publishes what he knows, his career is over. *(Beat)* Maybe more than his career.

KEVIN: Well. That's unpleasant. *(Beat)* Are you through?

FOGARTY: If you want me to be.

KEVIN: There's more?

FOGARTY: How much do you need to know?

(KEVIN *stares at him. He seems uncertain and somehow exposed.*)

KEVIN: Even when I know what you're doing to me, you do it anyway.

FOGARTY: I'm sorry. I don't feel good about any of this.

KEVIN: *(Beat)* When are you leaving?

FOGARTY: When I'm told to.

KEVIN: Where are you going?

FOGARTY: Where I'm useful.

KEVIN: Why?

FOGARTY: Why? Why am I leaving?

(KEVIN *nods.* FOGARTY *seems troubled, perhaps even a bit ashamed.*)

FOGARTY: Questions have arisen concerning my job performance.

KEVIN: Um. Hurts, doesn't it? I get that from your man Phipps everyday.

(FOGARTY *smiles.* KEVIN *makes what might be called a "leap of trust".*)

KEVIN: You figure to be around a couple weeks?

FOGARTY: Depends on events.

KEVIN: Stop by my place before you go. We'll have a drink.

(FOGARTY *is taken aback.* KEVIN *is consulting a notebook.*)

KEVIN: Say, I don't know, I'm really under the gun here, a week from Saturday? November twenty-third? You free?

FOGARTY: I might be.

KEVIN: Supper. After the football game. Sixish?

FOGARTY: Thank you. That's very...generous of you.

(FOGARTY *stands there, looking at the floor, trying to decide whether to say anything else.*)

KEVIN: Yes?

FOGARTY: *(Reluctantly)* Tell your dad not to go to Vienna. *(Beat)* Tell him not to go to the airport. *(He reaches out to shake* KEVIN's *hand.)* Take a favor, give a favor.

(KEVIN *doesn't shake hands.* FOGARTY *nods, then exits.*)

(KEVIN *watches him go. Lights out. Scene.*)

Scene Eleven
Kevin's Apartment #3

(*From the blackout, sound of steady, relentless rain. Sound also of TV: the Funeral March from Beethoven's* Eroica. *Occasional somber murmur of commentators' voices, not particularly distinguishable.*)

(*It's around 8 P M. Saturday, November 23, 1963.* CLYDE *and* KEVIN *sit transfixed in front of the cheap little T V watching the tragic playing out of events following the assassination the day previous of John F Kennedy.*)

(DARLA *passes in and out of the scene, usually with some cooking implement in hand. She'll glance at the screen, mutter some expression of sorrow, then exit off into kitchen.*)

(*A couple empty wine bottles are in evidence, but the guest of honor,* FOGARTY, *is nowhere to be seen.*)

DARLA: Oh that poor, poor woman. I could just die for her. *(She exits to kitchen)*

KEVIN: *(Beat)* I feel ashamed.

CLYDE: Not me, boy. I feel like about ninety seconds alone with Lee Oswald. That look on his face, that smug proud little face. I'd like to just stomp the shit out of him.

KEVIN: Fogarty was right. Again.

CLYDE: How so?

KEVIN: He told me there'd be a catastrophe before the year was out.

CLYDE: That doesn't exactly make him Nostradamus.

KEVIN: What's happening to this country? Puny little shits with guns, killing men better than them.

CLYDE: "Something wicked this way comes."

KEVIN: Clyde? Quoting Shakespeare? I'm stunned.

CLYDE: Shakespeare? I thought it was Ray Bradbury.

(DARLA *pops in from the O S kitchen.*)

DARLA: Where is that guy? He's two hours late! I'm starving and everything's burned! Why am I cooking for him anyway? I don't even like the little creep.

KEVIN: I'll call him again if you want. He's not answering. He's probably heading over here.

CLYDE: Maybe he stopped to pick up some wine. (*Inspecting an empty bottle*) And boy, I sure hope so.

DARLA: Oh God, that poor woman. Please turn that thing off. I can't take any more.

(*She exits back into kitchen.* CLYDE *glances at* KEVIN.)

CLYDE: I'm with her.

(KEVIN *concurs, turns off T V. Kill sound*)

CLYDE: I'm hungry. I admit it.

(KEVIN *dials up* FOGARTY, *listens, hangs up, shrugs.*)

CLYDE: I'm not surprised, really. I couldn't see Fogarty coming over here. I can't see him going anywhere. He seems like such a recluse.

KEVIN: Darla? Let's eat. To hell with him.

(KEVIN *exits to kitchen as* DARLA *re-enters.)*

DARLA: What a waste of effort. *(She flops onto sofa next to* CLYDE *and sulks.)*

CLYDE: Sorry, Darla.

DARLA: *(Regards him)* You must think I'm a real bitch.

CLYDE: Me? Why? Why would I—?

DARLA: Every time you come around you catch me in a rotten mood. I'm not like that. I'm a happy person, mostly.

CLYDE: I know that, Darla. Hey, I've been meaning to congratulate you. Kevin tells me you're a finalist in another beauty contest?

DARLA: Miss Military Ball. They announce it at the big dance. One week from tonight.

CLYDE: You like your chances?

DARLA: Well, some days I'm more confidant than others. Right now, today, I'm thinking I may be a little too short to win. All the other girls are these big tall things.

CLYDE: Well...

DARLA: The other way to look at that is, maybe my height will set me apart. Make me stand out, you know, in a favorable way.

CLYDE: I'll bet it will. *(Beat)* And that audition you had? For the movie, the documentary thing? How'd that go?

(DARLA*'s instantly in a lousy mood again, jumps up off the couch.)*

DARLA: Oh, go ask Rock Hudson over there!

(Said as KEVIN *enters carrying a couple bowls of ravioli. She exits past him in a snit.* CLYDE'*s baffled.)*

CLYDE: Now what'd I say?

KEVIN: Centron Studios audition. Sore subject.
(Hands CLYDE *a bowl)*

CLYDE: She didn't get cast?

KEVIN: Worse. *(Beat)* I did.

CLYDE: You?

KEVIN: Her car was busted. I drove. They saw me sitting around, threw a couple pages at me, and asked me to read. *(Beat)* The rest, like the Bay of Pigs, is history.

CLYDE: You're gonna be in a movie?

KEVIN: Well. An educational film.

CLYDE: And you didn't tell me? You punk! Who do you play?

KEVIN: A guy, you know, just a kid like me. Well. Maybe not exactly like me. It's stupid.

CLYDE: Say a line. Say one of your lines.

KEVIN: O K. *(A moment to get into character)* "I don't know what her name was. I can't remember."

CLYDE: *(Impressed)* Wow. That's pretty good.

KEVIN: I did what I could with it.

CLYDE: What's it called, this thing?

KEVIN: *Pay the Piper*. It's kind of a message film.

CLYDE: Like *The Seventh Seal*?

KEVIN: Well...shorter.

CLYDE: What's the message?

KEVIN: Don't have sex unless you wanna get syphilis.

CLYDE: Whew. That's raw.

KEVIN: I'm practically the hero. Well, maybe I'm the villain, I'm not sure. I only saw my two pages. I get interrogated by a health official. Some guy trying to get the name of all the girls I've slept with, see, because I'm a carrier.

CLYDE: You've got syphilis?

KEVIN: Right. And I've slept with so many girls I can't remember all their names. So the girls are out there, roaming around, you know? Infected, and loose.

CLYDE: So you're like...Typhoid Mary?

KEVIN: I was going for James Dean.

CLYDE: Kevin O'Rourke. Sexual predator.

KEVIN: Hey, they paid me seventeen dollars. For just two hours.

CLYDE: *(A brainstorm)* Kevin—I'm gonna get my dad to tell his Sex Ed Committee about this. Maybe they'll show it in the high schools around here. You'll be famous!

KEVIN: I wouldn't mind.

(Sound: phone rings)

KEVIN: I'll bet that's Fogarty. *(Answers it)* Hello? Who? Oh. Yeah, just a minute, I'll get her. Darla!

DARLA: *(O S)* Who is it?

KEVIN: I don't know. Some girl.

CLYDE: *(To* KEVIN*)* One of your sex slaves...

(Enter DARLA.*)*

DARLA: This is Darla. Oh, hi Mary Beth. Heard? Heard what? *(Beat)* Oh no. Tell me this isn't happening to me.

(Beat) This is so unfair. Is there another date? *(Beat)* Oh, this has just been the worst day of my life, Mary Beth. Can't talk, gotta go, bye. *(She hangs up, stands there, stunned.)*

KEVIN: Are you O K?

DARLA: They cancelled the Ball!

KEVIN: I'm sorry, what—?

DARLA: The Military Ball, Kevin! It's over. No dance, no Queen, over! All because of this stupid.. assassination!

(She runs off-stage. KEVIN *and* CLYDE *look at each other.)*

CLYDE: *(Without irony)* I know how she feels. They cancelled the football game, too.

*(*DARLA *re-enters, pulling on her winter coat, grabbing her purse and umbrella.)*

DARLA: I hate this day! I'm punching out. Tell Froggy thanks for a great supper. Freeze all that stuff out there, you hear me Kevin? Don't you let all that hard work go bad.

KEVIN: O.K.

DARLA: And don't you forget, Kevin O'Rourke: Thanksgiving dinner with my parents at the Lodge. Don't even think about getting out of that!

*(*DARLA *exits, emphatically. There is a moment of thoughtful silence in her wake.)*

KEVIN: Thus spake Zarathustra.

CLYDE: I thought you were flying out to California to see your dad for Thanksgiving.

KEVIN: That got complicated. My mom wanted me to go to her place, not his.

*(*KEVIN *turns on the T V again. Sound: Same loop as before—*Eroica, *commentators)*

KEVIN: Besides, Dad's kind of nervous about airports these days.

CLYDE: Oh, you told him what Fogarty said? About Vienna?

KEVIN: Of course.

CLYDE: So. Dinner with Darla and her parents. Part of your cunning plan to break off this engagement?

KEVIN: It's a free meal. What else am I going to do for Thanksgiving, open a can of soup?

CLYDE: Come over to our place.

KEVIN: Thanks, Clyde, but...I don't think your mom likes me all that much.

CLYDE: Well. You shouldn't have said bad things about J Edgar Hoover.

KEVIN: *(Beat)* What I was thinking of doing, maybe going over to see Joanna at Topeka State.

CLYDE: Fun.

KEVIN: No, you're right, it's not a barrel of laughs, Clyde. But how would you like to spend Thanksgiving walled up in the insane asylum?

CLYDE: Kevin. There's loyalty. And there's...contagion.

(KEVIN *stares at him*)

CLYDE: She's a sick girl, Kevin.

KEVIN: *(A threat)* You can stop now.

CLYDE: You didn't make her sick, you can't make her better. *(Beat)* Look. I'm not Ann Landers. I'm just your friend, and I'm telling you, Kevin, you gotta be careful not to confuse pity with love.

(KEVIN *lets this pass. Crosses to phone, dials, listens, hangs up.*)

KEVIN: I think there's something wrong over there.

CLYDE: Fogarty's?

KEVIN: Yeah. He was really looking forward to coming here, you know? *(Beat)* I'm going over to check on him. You want to come?

CLYDE: *(Getting up to go)* Naw, I'm heading home. Crummy weather. Horrible day. *(Beat)* His place smells bad.

KEVIN: Yeah, I know. Smells like puke. *(Beat)* He's not well. Fogarty's not well at all.

(For a moment they both just stare at the T V.)

CLYDE: Why do you think they killed him? Castro?

KEVIN: Maybe the Bay of Pigs, yeah. More likely Vietnam. Kennedy, he saw where that was going. He didn't want any part of that. All that Domino Theory crap.

CLYDE: So what are you saying? Hawks had him killed?

KEVIN: Deep in the Heart of Texas.

CLYDE: I don't believe that.

KEVIN: "There are more things in Heaven and Hell, Horatio, than are dreamt of in your philosophy."

CLYDE: You're talking about a coup. In America. Get real.

KEVIN: Wait till Oswald starts singing. It'll all come out.

(KEVIN turns off the T V. Kill sound. They exit.)

(Scene)

Scene Twelve
Fogarty's Apartment, Laos, Moscow

(Detailed notes for the staging of this scene can be found in the "After Words"essay. What follows is a fairly close approximation of the original production's approach. The technical challenge is the smooth integration of a cinematic Voice Over technique with the theatricality of the live action. C Ds of the Hmong and Vietnamese dialogue are available upon request.)

(FOGARTY's apartment, same time as previous scene: night of November 23, 1963.)

(FOGARTY is recording his memoirs into a big Wollensack reel-to-reel tape recorder on the floor next to him. In his mind, he is in Laos on the Plain of Jars ["P D J"], reliving events from April into July of 1961. He's in his recliner, and he's wearing a bathrobe. He dictates into the recorder's mike.)

FOGARTY: Plain of Jars, Laos. End of the dry season, 1961. Landgrab before the ceasefire. North Vietnamese going nuts, pushing south hard. General Vang Pao retreats to Padong with two thousand Hmong. Lima Site Two goes hostile. I extract Jack Shirley and Ahern, but too late for Wally Moon and Ballenger. Kong Le's got 'em in Lat Houang. *(Beat)* Middle of May. Muong Ngat. Slaughter. In two days, no signs of life. Maybe three hundred Hmong, a dozen Thai. All dead.

(Sound: Phone rings. Rather than answer it, he picks up a foreign-looking pipe and lights it, inhaling in a way that does not suggest pipe tobacco. Phone stops after four rings. He continues recording.)

FOGARTY: Thirty May. Re-supplying Padong. Seven thousand N V A regulars beating the shit out of Vang Pao and his boys. One-oh-five howitzers against

slingshots. Filthy weather. Break in the clouds. I make a
dash for it. Kickers clear the ammo and we get the fuck
out of Dodge. In come Chuck Mateer and the Wiz in
their Choctaw. I don't see it happen. Just an orange
glow in the fog bank and rotors screaming. Then
silence. I can't even get back in to help.

(FOGARTY *can't seem to get out of the moment. He looks
sick. He struggles out of the recliner. He's trying to exit to
the O S bathroom. His motor control is shaky, and he is
murmuring words that do not and need not make a great
deal of sense at this time.*)

FOGARTY: Ndu Nyong... (*Sounds like "jew-young"*)
Evil thing... Cloud devil... You saw me. That day
you saw me.

(FOGARTY *stumbles off-stage. Lights, dim throughout the
scene to this point, go to blackout. Scene continues.*)

(*From out of the blackout, sound:* FOGARTY's *voice,
amplified, as if coming through a tape recorder.*)

FOGARTY: (*Voice*) Padong goes down June sixth.
Kennedy pulls the plug. Everybody out of the pool,
time to dee-dee-Mao out of Lao. But we can't go
without Ballenger and Moon. Gotta lift 'em outta
Lat Houang compound.

(*Lights up slowly on another world, an expressionistic vision
of a Laotian hell—greens, yellows, and a sky as if on fire.*)

(*Sound: a helicopter—whup-whup-whup-whup—faint at
first under* FOGARTY's *continuing pre-recorded voice.*)

FOGARTY: (*Voice*) We thought we could avoid some heat
if we came at 'em outta the north. I was supposed to
link up with another H-34 at Lima Six near Phou San,
then we both come down on 'em outta the P D J.
Mighta worked except for the monsoon.

(Sound of helicopter very loud now, then noises of disaster— crashing sounds, metal twisting, engines screaming as...)

(FOGARTY comes hurtling onto the stage with great violence. He lies motionless, silent.)

(He has a seeping head wound, an injured leg, and is drenched and dirty. Tattered khaki slacks, no shirt, no boots, maybe one sock half on.)

FOGARTY: *(Voice)* I was ferrying a five-man Thai recon unit, a three-man Special Forces quick-strike team, my co-pilot, and a Hmong radioman-scout. *(Beat)* Everybody died but me. *(Beat)* Some died fast. Some didn't.

(FOGARTY tries to crawl towards a puddle of water. He's not very successful.)

FOGARTY: *(Voice)* Later, I heard Sergeant Ballenger made it out of Lat Houang somehow. Captain Moon, he got shot trying to escape a month after my crash. I was really sorry to hear that. I feel some way like I let him down.

(The Capture: two Soldiers are involved in this. They are sharply distinguishable.)

(One is a Pathet Lao who can understand both Vietnamese and Hmong and who functions as a Translator for the other, a North Vietnamese Army regular—in Army-speak, the first is a "P L," the second an "N V A." The N V A is technically in charge but is linguistically dependant upon the P L comrade in this particular neck of the woods. It seems effective to cast a female P L and a male N V A but this is not an edict.)

(The P L is dressed in guerrilla-style black pajamas and wears a straw hat; she carries a sidearm. The N V A wears a drab green North Vietnamese Army uniform, perhaps with a thatch of weedy camouflage affixed to his helmet and his back. He carries a sharpened bamboo pole that can serve variously

*as a walking stick, a goad, a spear, or a punishing cane. Both
soldiers are slightly-built but brutally efficient. Neither is
particularly vicious, but they are hyper, frightened for their
own safety, wary of enemy survivors from* FOGARTY's *crash.)*

(They enter from opposite sides.)

P L: *Dung lai! Dung lai khong tao ban! (Stop. Stop or I shoot
you.)*

N V A: *Dung lai! Dung lai!*

(The P L *covers* FOGARTY *with her weapon while the
N V A puts a foot on his back and briskly slips a noose over*
FOGARTY's *head—something twiny, thin, and tough that
extends to a loop which binds his hands behind his back.
The* N V A *questions him as if* FOGARTY *could understand
Vietnamese—which, in fact, he can on a rudimentary level.)*

N V A: *Dong bon cua may dau? (Where are your comrades?)*

*(P L is looking nervously in all directions even as she
continues to cover* FOGARTY. *When he doesn't answer—
he's in great pain from his injuries—*N V A *strikes him
with bamboo stick and again demands...)*

N V A: *Dong bon cua may dau?*

(Again, all FOGARTY *can do is groan.* N V A *stands over
him and commands—)*

N V A: *Dung day! (Stand up)*

P L: *Dung day!*

(They drag FOGARTY *to his feet.)*

N V A: *Di! Di mau! (Move. Move quickly)*

P L: *Di mau, di mau!*

(They shove him. FOGARTY *falls down. This enrages them.)*

N V A: *(Overlapping with P L) Do hen! Dung day!
(Coward. Stand up)*

P L: *(Overlapping) Dung day! Do qui yeu hen! (Stand up. Weakling)*

(FOGARTY gets the gist of this clearly enough but he's too injured to comply.)

FOGARTY: I can't. I'm sorry. I'm hurt, I can't stand....

(The soldiers seem to understand. They look him over and assess his wounds. With brief gestures they quickly convey the sense to each other of, "He's too hurt to walk and too valuable to kill." They combine to get him to his feet— perhaps by slipping the bamboo stick through his bound arms behind his back and lifting—and drag him off-stage. One of FOGARTY's legs is completely useless; he's in agony.)

(Scene continues.)

(Lights change to suggest passage of time. Sound: recommend use at this point of "Asian" instrumental music. Layered over this cue, FOGARTY's voice on tape re-commences.)

FOGARTY: *(Voice)* We walked for days.

(At some point during the "walking" speech, N V A and P L enter with FOGARTY, who is now walking with the aid of an improvised crutch. Perhaps he falters for a moment and the P L assists him. In any case, no aggression is evident in them until they come to the [unseen] Hmong village below.)

FOGARTY: *(Voice. Continuing)* Up mountain trails. Along a river. Once I saw The Rock off to the northeast—Phou Pha Thi, the Sacred Mountain. I figured, Sam Neua City, that's where they're taking me. *(Beat)* The only time we ever stopped was when we came to a hill-tribe village, usually Hmong. Then I became Show and Tell Time.

N V A: *Dung lai! (Stop)*

(FOGARTY does.)

N V A: *Quy xuong! (Kneel down)*

(FOGARTY *is made to understand, forcibly, and he complies, painfully.*)

FOGARTY: *(Voice)* The Vietnamese had to tell the Laotian what to say to the Hmong about the cowardly American. Tough when there's no word for "American."

N V A: *(To P L) Day la mot ten My yeu hen. (Here is a coward American.)*

P L: *(Gesturing her confusion)* "My yeu hen?"

(*Frustrated, the* N V A *whacks* FOGARTY *with the bamboo stick, knocking him face forward onto the ground.* N V A *tries to think of a concept the Hmong villagers can comprehend.*)

N V A: *(To P L) No la con qui tan ac! (He's a wood devil.)*

P L: *(Nods, and translates it vigorously into Hmong) Dlang hang zjung! No me-nyua moh! Tu-a tay young nu-a! (Wood devil. Eats babies. Kill these things.)*

FOGARTY: *(Voice. Continuing)* They decided to call me a Wood Devil. Said I ate babies. Told them to kill us on sight.

(N V A *and* P L *roughly-for show, mostly-yank* FOGARTY *to his feet.*)

N V A: *Dung day! (Stand up)*

(*Once he's on his feet,* P L *points gun at him and commands—*)

P L: *Di mau! Di mau! (Move quickly)*

(*They exit. Brief blackout or other light change and music cue to indicate passage of time.*)

(*Scene continues.*)

FOGARTY: *(Voice. Continuing)* Accommodations varied. None of them were Four Star. One night they put me in

a fifty-five gallon oil drum and buried me in a hole
in the ground. Claustrophobia. Asphyxiation. No
mosquitoes, though.

(Lights up on FOGARTY, *stripped down to khaki-colored
boxer shorts and crammed into a bamboo "tiger cage".)*

FOGARTY: *(Voice. Continuing)* Once in a village near Nha
Khang they found a tiger cage for me. Impossible to lie
down. Impossible to stand. Mosquitos fed on me at
will. Plenty of air, though.

(The pre-recorded voice ends here. FOGARTY *now speaks
"live." The effect at this point is complete displacement,
both temporal and spatial.* FOGARTY *is contorted
excruciatingly in the bamboo cage, but the position strangely
mimics his "recliner" posture from the start of this scene.
In fact, his voice echoes that tone of recollection and intimacy,
and the sense is that he has "returned" to his apartment and
we are less in Laos than we are in his own mind, the visual
evidence notwithstanding.)*

FOGARTY: *("live")* The worst thing about being in a tiger
cage, apart from your posture, is that you think about
tigers. Did the cage smell like tigers? Would they get a
whiff, come round to investigate? Oh, I knew they were
in the neighborhood.

(Lights up on a different level. GARY *is in his own cage,
the cell in his Moscow prison. They can't see each other.
P L soldier faces D S on one side of* FOGARTY'*s cage and the
N V A faces U S on the other side: guard duty.)*

FOGARTY: There are any number of terrifying ways to
die, Gary, ways you can't even imagine until it's too
late. But to be eaten alive? What could be worse?

GARY: I couldn't reach the Destruct Button. Spinning
violently at seventy thousand feet. I couldn't eject.
It would have cut my legs off above the knee. So I blew

the canopy and just crawled out. Face mask froze over instantly. I couldn't see the ground.

FOGARTY: I ended up in a dirt hut outside Sam Neua. My leech wounds, they all got infected. They gave me stuff. I don't know what was in it. Dysentery, dengue fever. It gets unclear.

GARY: I fell for over for over four minutes before the drogue opened. They say I hit a free-fall speed over four hundred miles an hour. I blacked out way before that.

FOGARTY: I used to think of you, Gary. You freezing in Moscow. Me here, burning my brains out with the fevers. High Fliers, boy, that's us.

GARY: They said, "Say you're sorry. It's important to be sorry. If you don't, the Judge says we can shoot you." (*Beat*) I was sorry.

(*As* FOGARTY *speaks the following lines, the* N V A *offers him a paper document—a confession, we presume. As he speaks, he signs it and hands it back to the soldier.*)

FOGARTY: They said, "Sign this. Ask Prince. You sign, you go." I was dead to the world. Not Missing in Action. Dead. Sign this, they said. Let them know you're alive.

(*Lights fade out on* GARY. *Once* FOGARTY *signs the paper and hands it to the* N V A, *he and the* P L *woman lift the tiger cage off* FOGARTY. *He falls to his side, frozen in the same posture imposed on him by the cage, which the soldiers now carry off with them as they exit.*)

(*As the lights fade on* FOGARTY, *he may try to crawl. In his delirium, he seems to be pleading with someone unseen. The language in which he speaks is Hmong.*)

FOGARTY: *Taw...tawa mang zhoh-ah.* (*Wait...please slow up.*)

(*Blackout. End of scene*)

Scene Thirteen
Fogarty's Apartment #2

(In blackout transition, FOGARTY *can still be heard in the same moment.)*

FOGARTY: *(From blackout into lights up)* Lo Ma. Geng. Maw. Mang zhoh... *(Lo Ma. Tired. Sick. Slow up...)*

(We are back in FOGARTY's *apartment. He's stretched out on his floor, and* KEVIN *is kneeling over him, perhaps wiping his face with a damp cloth.)*

KEVIN: Fred? The ambulance is coming, Fred. Hang on.

*(*KEVIN *grabs* FOGARTY's *bathrobe from the recliner, covers him with it.)*

FOGARTY: *(Starting to come around)* Kevin?

KEVIN: Yeah, it's me.

FOGARTY: Where...? What place is—?

KEVIN: Your apartment, Fred. Your Super let me in.

(Helping him into his robe)

KEVIN: Can you get to your chair?

(With his assistance FOGARTY *struggles to his feet and collapses into the recliner)*

KEVIN: Jeez, you're on fire. Let me get you some water.

*(*KEVIN *exits briefly, re-enters with a glass of water, helps* FOGARTY *drink.)*

FOGARTY: *(Rummaging through his pill bottles on the end table)* Thanks. Sorry you see me like this.

KEVIN: What's your doctor's number? Let me call for you.

FOGARTY: No, no, I'll be all right. You say you called an ambulance?

(KEVIN *nods*)

FOGARTY: Oh god...cancel it, please.

KEVIN: Will you let me drive you?

FOGARTY: It's dengue fever. Nobody can do anything. These pills control it. (*Swallows some of them*) Please. Don't let them put me in a hospital.

(KEVIN *crosses to phone, dials.*)

KEVIN: Yes. I want to cancel the request phoned in from Horizon View Apartments. (*Beat*) I'm very sorry. (*Hangs up, takes a good look at Fogarty*) Just tell me one thing: Are you contagious?

FOGARTY: No. This is like malaria. You get it from mosquitos. Souvenir of Laos.

KEVIN: Laos. I heard you babbling about that. You were talking in tongues there for awhile. (*Trying to recall some sounds*) "Doong die? Doong lie?"

FOGARTY: Vietnamese. All my nightmares are in Vietnamese. Except for the part where I escape. That's always in Hmong. (*Beat*) I need something to eat.

KEVIN: Well, don't blame Darla.

FOGARTY: Darla? That was tonight?

KEVIN: Ravioli.

FOGARTY: Kevin, I'm sorry. Please apologize to her.

KEVIN: You got any soup in the house?

FOGARTY: (*Trying to get up*) I think so.

KEVIN: Sit tight, I'll find it. (*As he exits to O S kitchen*) I'm good at opening soup cans.

(While KEVIN *intermittently busies himself in the kitchen,* FOGARTY *spots his foreign-looking pipe in too-plain a view and attempts to conceal it. In his haste and confusion, he botches the job.)*

KEVIN: *(From O S)* Who's Melinda?

FOGARTY: Melinda? She's my daughter.

KEVIN: *(O S)* You had a nice chat with her. And someone named Gary? Who's that, your brother?

FOGARTY: Close enough.

KEVIN: *(Popping back in)* You got a lot of people banging around inside your head.

FOGARTY: Don't we all?

KEVIN: And the things you said about Phipps. Wow.

FOGARTY: Like what?

KEVIN: Oh, you cussed him out a blue streak.

FOGARTY: I did?

KEVIN: No. Just kidding. *(Beat)* It's kind of fun, isn't it? Knowing stuff about somebody, and they don't know what you know? I can see the attraction.

(He exits back into O S kitchen; he yells back from there.)
So you were a P O W, Fred? In Laos?

FOGARTY: Not officially. No war, no prisoner.

KEVIN: *(O S)* How'd you get out? A trade? Like for Powers?

FOGARTY: I don't want to talk about this stuff.

*(*KEVIN *re-enters carrying a bowl of soup.)*

KEVIN: Why not?

FOGARTY: Because you have no need to know.

KEVIN: Here. It's hot, be careful.

FOGARTY: *(Taking the soup)* Thank you, Kevin. You're a good man.

KEVIN: *(Dryly)* And the son of a good man, too, right? Kind of guy wants to make the old man proud. Remember that? *(Beat)* Is yours, do you think? Proud of you?

FOGARTY: I don't know, Kevin. He passed away when I was twelve. *(A brief, strained silence)* Is Kennedy dead?

KEVIN: *(A bit stunned)* Yes, Fred, he is. They shot him yesterday. *(Beat)* Jesus, how long have you been out?

FOGARTY: Well...I guess since yesterday.

KEVIN: But you knew he'd been shot?

FOGARTY: This is good soup.

(FOGARTY reaches over to radio on end table.

(Sound: somber classical instrumental such as a Bach cello suite.)

KEVIN: Why'd they kill him, Fred?

FOGARTY: "They?"

KEVIN: Oswald's handlers. You know the squirrelly little shit wasn't working alone.

FOGARTY: I do?

KEVIN: Anything else defies reason.

FOGARTY: Reason is timid. It's easily defied.

KEVIN: I loved Jack Kennedy. *(Beat)* The man knew how to tell a joke. *(Beat; coldly furious)* Then this...nothing, this...speck...removes him from the planet.

FOGARTY: *(Beat)* Events dwarf us, Kevin.

KEVIN: And woe betide well-doers, huh Fred? Am I quoting you accurately?

FOGARTY: It sounds like something I'd say, yes.

KEVIN: *(Beat)* Do you think someday someone will shoot my father?

FOGARTY: *(Considering it)* I don't think he's that important.

(To KEVIN'*s look)*

FOGARTY: It's not like he's a head of state.

KEVIN: What would have happened if he'd gone to the airport that day?

FOGARTY: *(Hesitating)* I think he'd have missed his flight. *(Pause)* Did you pass along our concerns about him publishing the Omega data?

KEVIN: You know what I did and didn't do.

FOGARTY: So...what did he say?

KEVIN: He said "Tell Fogarty to go fuck himself."

FOGARTY: Well. That seems harsh.

KEVIN: Every time you mention his name I start hating you all over again.

FOGARTY: You're the one who brought him up.

KEVIN: Big fuckin' war hero. High Flier.

FOGARTY: Probably time for you to go home now, Kevin.

KEVIN: The man was "like your father." Quote unquote.

FOGARTY: What is it you want from me?

KEVIN: An apology.

FOGARTY: For what?

KEVIN: For disgracing his good name.

FOGARTY: His politics did that, not me.

KEVIN: You broke up his marriage!

FOGARTY: No, Kevin.

KEVIN: You leaked sleazy little stories about him. You made it sound like he screwed every co-ed who ever took a class from him.

FOGARTY: I did no such thing, Kevin.

KEVIN: Somebody did.

FOGARTY: All that's over.

KEVIN: Not for him. Not for me.

FOGARTY: Don't pursue this. Nobody needs to know everything about anyone.

KEVIN: You have me so confused. Part of me wants to be your friend, believe it or not. Sit around listening to you tell war stories. Another part of me feels bad for you. Cause you're not a spy, Fred, if that's how you see yourself. That's too dignified. You're just an informer. A snitch. Yet you seem like a decent man. It baffles me, how you could sink so low.

FOGARTY: Because I couldn't fly anymore! Because I needed two more years till I was vested for retirement. Because I'm smart enough to pass whatever course they need me to take. Is that enough? How many excuses would it take for you to say, "Oh well, that's all right then"?

KEVIN: Is that enough for you, Fred?

FOGARTY: The only excuse I ever needed was this: "Because I love my country."

KEVIN: So does my father, you asshole!

(Sound: phone rings. Once. KEVIN grabs it.)

KEVIN: (Vehemently) Fogarty's! (He listens for a second, then hangs up.)

FOGARTY: Wrong number?

KEVIN: Maybe.

FOGARTY: Did they identify themselves?

KEVIN: No.

FOGARTY: Did they say anything?

KEVIN: Yes. They said "Report for duty."

FOGARTY: That's it?

KEVIN: That's it. Click. Dial tone.

(FOGARTY is not thrilled. Resigned and exhausted is all.)

FOGARTY: I need to get cleaned up. Can you help me out of this chair?

(When KEVIN reaches out, FOGARTY seizes his hand with something like desperation.)

FOGARTY: On June 16th 1961 I crashed a Choctaw into the side of a Laotian mountain called Phou San. I killed ten men. I failed to die. Do you know why?

(KEVIN shakes his head "No")

FOGARTY: Neither do I. *(He pulls himself out of the chair; wobbly but standing.)* Do you know why my employers lost interest in you?

KEVIN: Because I've served whatever tiny little purpose I may once have had?

FOGARTY: No, Kevin. It's because you have no wound yet, no hole in your heart for them to fill. Absent that, how can they own you?

(FOGARTY exits for his off-stage bathroom. KEVIN's feeling somewhat drained himself. He plops down in the recliner. He spots FOGARTY's strange-looking pipe.)

(He sniffs it curiously. It's possible to cut past the next moment to the results at the start of the next scene. Or it's possible to show KEVIN furtively lighting up, once. The effect

is to sort of physically liquefy him. He ends up, quickly,
as a heap on the floor.)

(Blackout. End of scene)

Scene Fourteen
Fogarty's Apartment #3

(Sound cues from blackout: the Bach cello suites that played
through the latter half of the previous scene now give way to
a recognizable but only dimly audible T V newscast loop.
It is eleven A M, Sunday, 24 November 1963. Cronkite and
others are covering on-going events in the Dallas police
station.)

(Add sound of phone ringing as lights up on KEVIN stretched
out on the floor, sleeping, a pillow under his head, a blanket
covering him. The apartment looks cleaner.)

(Two overnight bags sit near the door to the street.)

(FOGARTY enters, now well-dressed in early sixties casual.
He steps over KEVIN to get to the phone.)

FOGARTY: Fogarty's. (*His conversation is low-keyed,*
conscious of KEVIN's *presence.*) Yes sir, good morning.
(*Beat*) Understood. Do we have an E T D yet? Copy.
And the driver? I'm ready now, yes sir. (*Pause*) Do you
think that will be necessary? I understand. Cleveland.
Very well. Yes, I'm fine, thank you. Yes sir. You too, sir.

(He hangs up. He looks anxious as he processes what he's
heard. KEVIN stirs.)

FOGARTY: Are you O K?

(KEVIN looks around, disoriented.)

FOGARTY: I'll get you some orange juice. Then you've
got to get out of here.

(KEVIN *more or less crawls into the recliner as* FOGARTY *exits and re-enters with a glass of juice.*)

KEVIN: Boy, was I having some weird dreams.

FOGARTY: *(Unsmiling)* I don't doubt it. *(Beat)* I don't appreciate what you did.

KEVIN: What? Fall asleep?

FOGARTY: Don't be cute. *(Beat)* Keep your hands off my property.

(KEVIN *pauses, then nods "O K"*)

KEVIN: What was that stuff?

FOGARTY: Medicine. For my headaches.

KEVIN: Was that marijuana?

FOGARTY: No.

KEVIN: I'll bet it was.

FOGARTY: *(Losing it a bit)* The point is, you don't know what it was and you smoked it anyway, you dumb shit.

KEVIN: If it wasn't marijuana, what was it?

FOGARTY: Opium.

KEVIN: Opium? *(Thinks about it)* Where'd you get it, Kansas City?

FOGARTY: No, Kevin. I got it in Vientiane, Laos. Go to the Hotel Royale and ask for Pierre. Tell him Freddy the Fog sent you.

KEVIN: *(Self-diagnosing)* Interesting. I don't feel sick or hung-over... *(To* FOGARTY *by way of explanation)* I'm researching non-alcoholic intoxicants.

FOGARTY: How amusing. *(Beat)* You know what I am, Kevin? I'm a drug addict. *(Beat)* I throw up at least twice a day.

KEVIN: *(A bit embarrassed, a bit shocked)* You don't look the type, Fred.

FOGARTY: Well according to you, I don't look like a pilot, either. *(Beat)* You kids get all your information from movies.

KEVIN: You don't have to be such a grouch. *(Indicating the overnight bags)* Your transfer came through?

FOGARTY: No, not yet. Oh, the bags? I thought you meant...I've got papers in for re-assignment to Laos.

KEVIN: You want to go back there?

FOGARTY: Desperately.

KEVIN: Where they sending you instead?

FOGARTY: *(Hesitates)* Cleveland.

KEVIN: Cleveland. *(Beat)* Jewel of the East. *(Beat)* Dare I ask why?

FOGARTY: Medical procedure.

KEVIN: Serious?

FOGARTY: I'm having a wart removed from my ass. Speaking of which... *(He crosses to street door exit, motioning for Kevin to use it.)* You've gotta hit the road. So do I.

KEVIN: *(Indicating)* I'm waiting for Oswald. Cronkite's saying they're bringing him through for the arraignment any minute now.

FOGARTY: Cripes, you're harder to get rid of than my bathroom mold.

KEVIN: Your bathroom is pretty rank, Fred. Speaking in my professional janitorial capacity.

FOGARTY: *(Crossing towards O S kitchen)* If my driver comes while you're still here, there's the back door. Use it. *(He exits briefly.)*

KEVIN: Are you really going under the knife, Fred?

FOGARTY: *(From O S)* Looks that way. Just an
exploratory. *(He re-enters with two cups of coffee.)*

FOGARTY: Possible tumor. Probably benign.
(Handing KEVIN *a mug)* Careful, it's hot.

KEVIN: *(Taking coffee)* Lungs?

FOGARTY: Brain, actually.

*(*KEVIN *reacts.)*

FOGARTY: I have a plate in my skull. It's been the source
of some problems.

KEVIN: *(After studying him intently)* Freddy the Fog.
You disappear right before my eyes.

FOGARTY: Say what you mean.

KEVIN: Your whole life sounds like a lie.

FOGARTY: Kevin, you're twenty years old and you're
living in Kansas. You couldn't recognize the truth if it
bit you in the behind.

KEVIN: Maybe not, Fred. But I'm a quick study. *(Beat)*
Where are you going really? And please don't tell me
Cleveland.

FOGARTY: What difference does it make what I say?
It's all the same to you—lies and damn lies.

KEVIN: Being around you will do that to a body.

FOGARTY: Courage is not a lie. Or compassion.
(Hesitates, staring at KEVIN, *then decides. From a drawer
in the end table, he retrieves a boxed seven inch reel of tape.)*
I want you to hold this for me for a couple of days.
Just till I get back.

KEVIN: What's this? A tape?

FOGARTY: Sort of my...memoirs. If anybody cares.

(KEVIN *is discomforted.*)

FOGARTY: This will sound odd, I suppose, but... may I say I've enjoyed talking with you?

KEVIN: I don't get this. What's going on?

FOGARTY: I'm sorry for any harm I've done you. And please, stay in school, whatever you do.

KEVIN: You're talking like a dead man. Are you aware of that?

FOGARTY: (*Smiles*) All week long I've had this... recurring thought...mocking me. "The paths of glory lead but to the grave." I can't place it.

KEVIN: That's from your favorite poem, Fred. "Full many a—?"

FOGARTY: "Flower."

KEVIN: "—is born to blush unseen, And waste its—?"

FOGARTY: "Sweetness."

KEVIN: "—on the desert air." Nice adjustment.

FOGARTY: I'm a quick study. (*Beat*) Have you ever heard of Rudolph Anderson?

KEVIN: No. Should I have?

FOGARTY: Not if we're doing it right. (*Beat*) He was a High Flier, Kevin.

KEVIN: A U-2 guy?

FOGARTY: Shot down over Cuba during the missile crisis last year.

KEVIN: And they kept that quiet?

FOGARTY: (*Almost gently*) Whole wars are being fought you know nothing about.

KEVIN: "Plausible deniability." Like Ike tried with Francis Gary Powers.

FOGARTY: It's a concept that works until it doesn't, yes.

KEVIN: I'm having a horrible thought here, Fred. Are you telling me you're going back up in one of those things? Those U-2s? *(Silence)* You said they wouldn't let you fly any more. Didn't you? Or was that just another lie?

FOGARTY: Necessity is the Mother of Retention. *(Smiles)* This is a fluke. I'm probably a back-up's back-up.

KEVIN: Don't you have to pass a physical or something?

FOGARTY: This isn't spring football practice, Kevin.

KEVIN: But you can hardly stand.

FOGARTY: They let us fly sitting down.

KEVIN: To Cuba?

FOGARTY: That would be my guess, given the Kennedy assassination.

KEVIN: What should I feel about this? Are you scared?

FOGARTY: Interesting question. *(Beat)* Do you know what a SAM-2 is?

KEVIN: A missile of some kind?

FOGARTY: Russian surface-to-air, yes. They can reach us at maximum elevation. Powers proved that. Major Anderson confirmed it. *(Beat)* The fascinating thing about missiles, Kevin, is that they're not bullets. When a bullet misses you, it just keeps right on going. When a SAM-2 misses you, you think, "Thank God, I'm saved!" Then you look out your canopy and watch the son of a bitch do a one-eighty and come right back at you. You zig, you zag, then poof. *(Beat)* The grace of God is contingent.

KEVIN: Fred. I've got an idea. Don't go.

FOGARTY: What?

KEVIN: You heard me. Call in sick. Forge a note from your mother. Stay home from school, Fred.

FOGARTY: I can't do that. Are you crazy?

KEVIN: Go stand in front of a mirror, will you? Take a look at yourself. It's time to move on, Fred.

FOGARTY: This is my last flight.

KEVIN: The last flight is the flight every dead pilot died on. Here's the difference: They didn't know it would be their last. You do. Fred, it's simple. Scrub it.

FOGARTY: You shouldn't tell me such things! You shouldn't play to my weakness. (*Beat*) Don't you realize how bad they must need me? To call on me? I am the bottom of the barrel. You think I don't know that? That's how bad they need me. (*Beat*) If I do well on this mission, maybe they'll let me go back to Laos. Vang Pao's re-grouped at Long Cheng. I could really be of use there, Kevin. With the Hmong people? I need to be there.

KEVIN: Is that what they're dangling? To get you back up in that spy plane? (*Beat*) You just told me what you are to your bosses. Deniable. Dispensable. Replaceable. (*Sinking*) Everything is replaceable. Girlfriends. Kennedy. You and me. My dad. (*Beat*) The world's a vicious place. Nothing is what it seems. Nothing lasts.

FOGARTY: You're getting on my nerves. Why don't you go write a poem or something?

(*Sound: phone rings. Once, twice at most, before* FOGARTY *snatches it up.* KEVIN *becomes riveted by the T V. The sound of the newsmen at Dallas becomes more intelligible.*)

FOGARTY: Fogarty. Yes. Ten minutes? Can do. (*Beat*) Ready as I'll ever be.

(*He hangs up and turns to watch the T V.*)

KEVIN: There he is. Look at that little shit.

(Sound: on T V, a pistol shot and pandemonium.)

(KEVIN leaps straight out of his chair.)

KEVIN: Jesus! Jesus Christ! They shot Oswald!

(KEVIN is transfixed, hands to head, horrified. FOGARTY, on the other hand, seems oddly self-absorbed, watching dispassionately as if looking at a gangster movie.)

(Blackout. End of scene)

Scene Fifteen
Day Room, Topeka State Hospital #2

(Lights up on the cheap table and two formica chairs from the earlier Hospital scene.)

(It is Thanksgiving Day, 1963. For the moment CLYDE is alone, sitting stiffly, uncomfortably. A nicely-wrapped present sits on the table. There may be muted Sounds typical of hospital announcements—requests for certain doctors to go to certain places, etc.)

(CLYDE gets impatient and starts to come D S as if to ask a receptionist a question.)

VOICE: *(Nurse. As if through intercom, mildly amplified, directionally from back of house)* Please take your seat.

(CLYDE does so, a bit chastened. KEVIN soon enters and takes his place at the table.)

KEVIN: They're checking on her. Shouldn't be long.

(CLYDE starts reaming him out in a kind of church-voice whisper.)

CLYDE: Thanksgiving Dinner at Topeka State Hospital.

KEVIN: I really appreciate this, Clyde. She will, too.

CLYDE: Consider the ramifications. One. You are now *persona non grata* in my mother's house forever.

KEVIN: For sure.

CLYDE: Two. The next time Darla tracks you down, you better have an armed bodyguard.

KEVIN: We're over.

CLYDE: Three. I am now officially the best friend you will ever have in your entire, miserable life.

KEVIN: I already knew that, Clyde.

(CLYDE *relents somewhat. Picks up the gift-wrapped present.*)

CLYDE: So whacha bring her?

KEVIN: Book of poems. William Blake. It's got a bunch of his engravings. God. Angels. Heaven. (*As if apologizing*) She's always talking about Heaven.

CLYDE: (*Beat*) Fogarty back yet?

KEVIN: Not yet.

CLYDE: How long's it been?

KEVIN: A few days. Four. Four days.

CLYDE: Well. Could be anything.

KEVIN: I've been listening to that tape he left me.

CLYDE: Yeah?

KEVIN: The hell that man's been through. Like, talking about tape? You know what a tapeworm looks like?

CLYDE: Nasty, I'm thinking.

KEVIN: In Laos, when he was a P O W? Fogarty pulled a twenty-six foot long one out of his butt.

CLYDE: (*Grimacing*) Thanks for that image.

KEVIN: We have no idea about anything, Clyde.

CLYDE: (*Something O S catches his eye*) Hey. That orderly wants you.

(KEVIN *stands and starts to exit but they come to understand that it's* CLYDE *who's being summoned.* CLYDE *is a bit nonplussed but exits.* KEVIN *stares after him, waits nervously.)*

(CLYDE *re-enters no more than thirty seconds later. He looks grim.* KEVIN *stares at him.* CLYDE *can't meet his gaze. They don't move.)*

(*Lights dim to blackout. End of scene.*)

Scene Sixteen
The Alcove #3

(*Mid-December 1963, just prior to the Christmas break.* PHIPPS *is studying some report. He concludes it and starts to exit when* KEVIN *enters opposite him.* KEVIN *is dressed well in cold-weather apparel which contributes to* PHIPPS'S *inability to recognize him initially.)*

KEVIN: Dr Phipps? Have you got a moment, sir?

PHIPPS: Not really, but what can I do for you?

KEVIN: I'm Kevin O'Rourke.

PHIPPS: Ah. The janitor.

KEVIN: That's how I pay my tuition, sir, as you know.

PHIPPS: Didn't recognize you out of uniform.

KEVIN: I was hoping you'd have some information on Fred Fogarty? He disappeared about three weeks ago? Around the time of the assassination?

PHIPPS: How do his whereabouts concern you?

KEVIN: He's my friend.

PHIPPS: Really? I was unaware he had one.

KEVIN: It seems odd he'd disappear right before finals.

PHIPPS: Not at all. He's off researching his dissertation.

KEVIN: Oh? Where, exactly?

PHIPPS: Cleveland, I believe. Now if you'll excuse me?

KEVIN: I'm worried about his health, Dr Phipps. He indicated he might be in line for a surgical procedure. In Cleveland, actually.

PHIPPS: *(Considers Kevin before responding)* I'm sure you understand that such information, if I possessed it, would be strictly confidential in nature.

KEVIN: Is there a hospital? Any kind of forwarding address?

PHIPPS: You're an irritating young man, Mr O'Rourke.

KEVIN: Could you just tell me, is he safe?

PHIPPS: Safe? I don't know. I've never been to Cleveland. *(Starts to exit)*

KEVIN: You wouldn't hurt him, would you?

PHIPPS: What in God's name are you talking about?

KEVIN: He's terrified of you.

PHIPPS: Well. Fred had problems.

KEVIN: War wounds?

PHIPPS: War? You refer to...?

KEVIN: Laos.

PHIPPS: *(Beat)* There's no war in Laos.

KEVIN: Ah.

PHIPPS: Is there?

KEVIN: I don't know. I've never been to Laos.

PHIPPS: Shouldn't you be out swallowing goldfish, Mr O'Rourke? Or seeing how many of your friends can stuff themselves into a phone booth?

KEVIN: Fred told me things.

PHIPPS: No doubt. That was one of his problems.
A condition I diagnose as diarrhea of the mouth.
It's epidemic around here. Your father was so afflicted.
Let's hope it's not genetic.

KEVIN: Why was it a good thing he left when he did?
My father? Do you recall telling me that?

PHIPPS: Don't get me started.

KEVIN: You used Fred Fogarty to destroy my father.

PHIPPS: Your father's a traitor. And, may I add? —a
philanderer. Not a very discriminating one, either, to be
frank. But don't take my word. Go ask your Mommy.

KEVIN: You're a liar. A filthy liar.

PHIPPS: I don't know how to lie. Other than by not
revealing. I'm quite good at that. I covered up for your
father for years. Right up until I perceived that he was
becoming a threat to my country with his insanely
naïve political rants. And apropos of that, give him
a message for me the next time you chat, will you?
Remind him that Omega means The End. Will you
do that for me?

KEVIN: Poor Fred. He told me once, we all have a
choice. We can soar with the eagles, or we can slither
around with the snakes.

PHIPPS: Let's touch base with reality here, shall we?
I'm the best friend Fogarty ever had. I personally
secured this little sinecure for him. As inept as he
was. As damaged. And finally, as repellent and
compromised as he became. And why did I go out
of my way to do that for him, Kevin? Why did I put
my dick on the chopping block for Freddy the Fog?

KEVIN: Because you knew there was a hole in his heart.

PHIPPS: Oh, don't get literary on me. *(Beat)* I did it
because Fred Fogarty was a brave man in spite of

himself. Once upon a time he flew higher than any man who ever lived. That much is verifiable. Everything else you have on that tape? Never happened.

KEVIN: *(Pause)* You know about the tape?

PHIPPS: I do now. *(Beat)* It's of no consequence. The sad, delusional babblings of a broken-down man in the terminal stages of brain cancer.

KEVIN: That's nothing but a cover story.

PHIPPS: Is it? Because if it is, I think it's a damn good one. *(Beat)* May I leave you with one thought, Kevin, for I really must toddle off now. Life's hardest lesson. Do you know what it is?

KEVIN: Love thy neighbor as thyself?

PHIPPS: Never bought into that one, Kevin. Too many variables. No, Life's Hardest Lesson? Silence is Golden. Or as my father used to say, Loose lips sink Phipps. *(Smiles)* Have yourself a Merry Little Christmas, Kevin. Regards to your Pop.

(PHIPPS *exits. Lights down on* KEVIN *to blackout. End of Scene)*

Scene Seventeen
Kevin's Apartment #4

(In blackout transition, isolate FOGARTY's *Wollensack reel-to-reel, now in* KEVIN's *apartment. Sound mimics the on-stage source but is subtly amplified.* KEVIN *remains O S initially.)*

FOGARTY: *(Voice)* You're riding inside a thin aluminum skin. It's sixty below zero outside. One-tenth the atmospheric pressure you need to survive. Tear your flight suit, your blood boils.

(Lights up on rest of apartment area.)

FOGARTY: *(Voice)* Twenty-five thousand feet below, you've got an escort—thirty MiGs waiting for you to flame out and drop within range. You can't see them. You just feel the hairs on your neck stand up.

(KEVIN *enters with a sandwich and a glass of milk, settles on couch, listening intently.)*

FOGARTY: *(Voice)* Down on the ground, if you could see it, it'd be like watching somebody flicking a Zippo lighter. Little flames. Flick. Flick. Flick. Then little red streaks, like fingers pointing up at you. *(Beat)* I live with a sense of doom now. Other people smell it, and avoid me.

(KEVIN *stops tape, then fast forwards it. There's a muffled knock on* KEVIN's *door. He's startled and hurriedly conceals the tape recorder, perhaps with a blanket.)*

KEVIN: Who's there?

CLYDE: It's Cassius Marcellus Clay, and on the count of four, I'm gonna beat down your door.

(KEVIN *crosses to door, unlocks it, and* CLYDE, *in heavy winter gear, bursts through.)*

CLYDE: What you locking your doors for? You think thieves go out in weather like this?

KEVIN: This tape is making me paranoid. *(Indicating something* CLYDE's *carrying)* What's that?

CLYDE: Happy New Year. *(Thrusts a bottle of champagne at him and throws off his heavy coat and gloves, makes himself at home.)*

KEVIN: French champagne.

CLYDE: My first legally-purchased bottle of booze, Kevin. I have at last attained my majority. *(Striking a pose)* You are looking at the full flowering of my manhood.

KEVIN: That's a disgusting thought.

CLYDE: Go open that nectar, my friend, and let me introduce you to The Good Life.

(KEVIN *exits to O S kitchen as* CLYDE *rummages through records, selecting a Beatles. Sound: [You Really Got a]* Hold On Me.)

CLYDE: You going to the U C L A game Tuesday?

KEVIN: *(O S)* Naw, they're gonna kill us. I got enough pain in my life.

CLYDE: Dick Gregory's coming to the Aud. You're set for that, right?

KEVIN: *(O S)* I don't know...I'm thinking about it.

(Sound: if timing can be managed, of champagne cork)

CLYDE: C'mon man, quit hibernating in here. You can't let winter turn you into a pussy.

KEVIN: *(Enters, with glasses and bottle)* I hate New Year's. Makes me think too much.

CLYDE: Well, if you hadn't kissed off Darla, you could be out right now dancing the foxtrot at the Lodge.

KEVIN: *(Smiles)* Foxtrot... *(Beat)* Place does seem emptier without her.

CLYDE: What do you miss the most, the naughty massages?

KEVIN: *(Thoughtfully)* The lasagna, I think. *(Beat)* There was something sweet about her, though. She grew on me.

(KEVIN *lapses into silence.* CLYDE *knows what he's thinking and tries to forestall it.)*

CLYDE: Get your mind off that.

KEVIN: I can't.

CLYDE: Try harder.

KEVIN: How could they have let her do that inside of a damn hospital?

CLYDE: They can't be everywhere at once all the time, Kevin.

KEVIN: Three days before they were gonna let her out.

CLYDE: Well, that's the key, isn't it? "Out"? "Out" scared her.

KEVIN: I keep thinking how Joanna looked three years ago, swanning around in the backseat of a convertible with all the other Homecoming Queen candidates. Bare shoulders. Corsage. *(Beat)* Probably turn out to be the happiest night of my life, and I pissed it away without a thought.

CLYDE: You didn't piss it away. You're still thinking about it.

KEVIN: How can things go so wrong so fast?

CLYDE: My mother's a gardener. When she sees the first few shoots taking off, she doesn't pay them a glance. She knows they're gonna die. First ones shoot up too fast. They wilt in the sun, they droop, they're gone. Nothing you can do, Kev. *(A brief pause as he fills the wine glasses)* You've gotta drink this stuff right away, or it goes flat. What shall we toast?

KEVIN: To a better day tomorrow.

CLYDE: God, you have such low expectations.

KEVIN: I'm Irish.

CLYDE: To the World! We have you in our sights. Surrender now or we will take you by force. *(Beat)* I'm German.

(They drink.)

KEVIN: This is good, Clyde.

CLYDE: Yeah, and the more you drink, the better it gets. *(Beat; indicates tape recorder)* Listening to Fogarty's tape again?

(KEVIN *nods;* CLYDE *gives way to mild irony)*

CLYDE: Great way to beat the blues, huh?

KEVIN: It fascinates me. It's like listening to somebody who went over Niagara Falls in a barrel.

(KEVIN *hits "play" on recorder. Sound:* FOGARTY'*s voice)*

FOGARTY: *(Voice)* Once I flew a plane so high that I saw the sky turn black all around me and the stars at noon. No sound. Just my breathing. And I felt something watching me. Something malevolent. I was trespassing. I plummeted to earth. It was too late. Ndu Nyong had seen me.

(KEVIN *turns off tape.)*

CLYDE: What's he saying? "Jew Young"?

KEVIN: Sounds like that. It's the Devil. The Hmong people think it lives on top of the highest mountain. Fogarty believes it's tracking him personally.

CLYDE: Like he's cursed?

KEVIN: Where he ended up, what they had him doing? Wheatland? This was Hell for him.

CLYDE: Where do you think he is now, Kevin?

KEVIN: That's what haunts me.

CLYDE: And which was the cover story?

KEVIN: You mean the brain surgery in Cleveland?

CLYDE: Did that cover a U-2 Cuba mission? Or was Cuba a cover to get him into a hospital in Cleveland?

KEVIN: He was scared to death of hospitals...

CLYDE: And here's the biggie: Is he dead or alive?

KEVIN: I feel he's dead.

CLYDE: Maybe his transfer came through. Maybe he re-deployed to Laos?

KEVIN: He left here a dead man, Clyde. By what force or at whose hands...

(Sound: phone ringing. KEVIN *crosses to it.)*

CLYDE: If it's Darla begging you to come back, be strong.

KEVIN: Hello? Oh, hi. *(His voice slips into neutral; almost affectless)* Yeah, Happy New Year's. Where you calling from? Sorry, forgot. Can't ask that, can I? *(Beat)* No, just hanging around with a buddy of mine. Darla? No, we broke up, remember? Yeah. Well, it happens. As you know.

CLYDE: Ask him about Phipps.

KEVIN: I don't know, Dad. I'm kinda up in the air about that. I'm just so sick of school. *(Beat)* Yes, I know you have good friends in Toronto. You're getting way ahead of yourself here, Dad. Calm down, O K? The draft is not a death sentence, and you didn't raise me to be a coward. *(Beat; then, a bit wearily)* No, I know conscientious objectors aren't—look, I've got guests, I have to get going, O K? Yeah. You too. Bye. *(He hangs up, exasperated.)*

CLYDE: How come you didn't ask him about Phipps?

KEVIN: Because my head's ready to explode, Clyde!

CLYDE: Ah.

*(*KEVIN *finishes off the champagne)*

KEVIN: I can't stand talking to him anymore.

CLYDE: Really? Your dad? *(Beat)* Can I ask why?

KEVIN: No.

CLYDE: Can I ask something else?

KEVIN: No.

CLYDE: Thanks. What happened on the Omega war games research? Is he going into print with that?

KEVIN: Publisher got scared. Killed it. Dad's thinking of suing for breach of contract.

CLYDE: They got to them on the other end, huh? *(Looking closely at Kevin, who seems, inexplicably, to be near tears)* You O K, Kevin?

KEVIN: Not really, no.

CLYDE: Is it the champagne?

KEVIN: No. I like the champagne.

CLYDE: I got another bottle out in the car.

KEVIN: You do?

CLYDE: Yeah. Let's go cruising. Pick up some chicks.

KEVIN: It's ten below zero on New Year's Eve, Clyde. The only thing we're gonna pick up is a drunk driving ticket.

CLYDE: C'mon, you need some fresh air. *(Looking around)* This place is starting to smell like Fogarty's.

KEVIN: Maybe I should hire a maid.

CLYDE: Ja. A Svedish maid. Mit der big ɔoobies. *(He's got his coat back on and is heading out the door.)* Don't make me have to come back in here and get you, O'Rourke.

(CLYDE EXITS. As KEVIN gathers his winter stuff to join him...)

(Lights X-fade to Bluebell Lake.)

(Scene)

Scene Eighteen
Bluebell Lake #3

(KEVIN *and* CLYDE *standing on the pier in parkas and gloves, freezing. They pass a bottle of champagne back and forth once before* CLYDE *announces...*)

CLYDE: I'd like to think I'm the kinda guy you could drop off above the Arctic Circle with just a compass and a knife, and I'd make it back alive. (*Pause*) I'd like to think that.

KEVIN: Clyde, you're still living at home with your mom and dad.

CLYDE: Can I help it if I was improperly weaned? In my heart, I'm a Wilderness Guide.

KEVIN: How's your dad doing? I read he got roughed up at the Board of Ed riot.

CLYDE: Pulled a hamstring. (*Beat*) No fun facing down a roomful of raging Baptists. Just so some gym teacher can say "vagina."

(KEVIN *has become "broody" again;* CLYDE *has to prompt him.*)

CLYDE: You gotta snap out of this, Kevin.

KEVIN: This past six months...

CLYDE: Six months ago we were bitching that nothing ever happens around here.

KEVIN: What if it's true, Clyde? All the lies Phipps put out about my dad? What if he really was sleeping with every co-ed on this campus?

CLYDE: Well, if he's getting it all, that would explain why the rest of us aren't getting any.

KEVIN: You joke, yeah, but how would you feel if it was your dad?

CLYDE: Incredulous. Then, proud as a peacock.

KEVIN: I'm sure.

CLYDE: C'mon, don't let them mess with you this way. You'll go psycho.

KEVIN: I just wish I knew where I was gonna be six months from now.

CLYDE: Why don't we join the Army? Beat 'em to the punch?

KEVIN: Yeah, you'd look good in a tank.

CLYDE: I was thinking more like Cooking School.

(Lights change. Moonlight on snow-covered lake effect.)

KEVIN: Wow. Look at that moon coming up. Like a big pregnant lady.

CLYDE: Think we'll ever get there? Like Kennedy wanted?

KEVIN: The Moon? I'd go. They wouldn't even have to pay me. *(Beat)* Any more champagne?

CLYDE: Maybe a swig apiece.

(KEVIN *takes the bottle, holds it up to the sky)*

KEVIN: To Freddy the Fog. Wherever you are, it's better than where you were. *(Drinks, hands it to C_YDE)* Give us a toast, Clyde. Something to warm my cold, cold heart.

CLYDE: *(lifting bottle to the sky)* To the Moon. Proof that what goes down, must come up. *(Smiles)* Even you, my friend. Even you.

(CLYDE *drinks the last of it. They stare out at the lake, at the moon, at the audience.)*

(Lights dim to blackout.)

END OF PLAY

AFTER WORDS

I began processing LAST DAYS OF THE HIGH FLIER
a long time ago. I finally hit the "Now or Never" barrier
in May 2001 and plunged in. I finished a rough draft
about two weeks before 9/11. When I could stand to
think about something as trivial as a play again, I read
what I had written, threw it away and started over.
That draft became the Production Script, the version
that premiered in 2004. As one does after a production,
I rewrote HIGH FLIER once again, striving mightily
to fix all its deficiencies, real, imagined, feared, or
potential. What you're reading is as close as I could
get to telling it right.
Dennis J Reardon , August 2004

Production Notes

If you're not a director, designer, or actor wondering
how to get LAST DAYS OF THE HIGH FLIER on its
feet, you probably shouldn't read any further.

Here's an alternative title that might help: KEVIN'S
LIFE, JUNE 1963 THROUGH NEW YEAR'S EVE 1963.
That life includes girlfriends, divorces, suicides,
assassinations, mysterious strangers, secret wars,
lifetime friendships, betrayals, and the lurking presence
of an increasingly ravenous evil. Kevin's point-of-view
is violated only three times—briefly at the tops of
Scenes Eight and Ten and again, emphatically, in Scene

Twelve, the Laotian nightmare. So Kevin's the focal point throughout, as you might expect from a tale of lost innocence—domestic, national, and global.

But Fogarty is why I had to write the play. He and Kevin twine about one another like strands of D N A. To say their relationship is ambiguous is to belabor the obvious. The most accurate analogy I can come up with is Big Brother, Little Brother, and on that level Fogarty finds himself ensnared in what can only be called a domestic drama centering around the ghostly departed Father. It's important to remember, I think, that— as sick and broken as he is—Fogarty is a combat pilot. Whoever plays this man should have an expansive mind. A wounded heart helps.

A word or two about Darla and Joanna. They are the flip side of each other. Together they form an odd romantic triangle with Kevin. It's 1963. One version of femininity is about to be severely challenged by another. If Darla is the alpha-female of her day— a goal-oriented young woman moving efficiently through her social matrix—Joanna is her darker sister, ahead of the cultural curve, alone, lost.

I view this period, accurately or not, as far less ironic than our own times. An actress attempting Darla should not play down to her. You may be hipper, more enlightened, and generally "superior" to her, but if you play that, you will go down in flames. Darla is a creature of light in a dark play, and audiences desperately need her.

Clyde is a living refutation of the big dumb jock/ big dumb hick canard. He's smarter than hell, and he knows just what he wants to do with his life. In fact, the "kids" in this play suggest a time suffused with great intellectual curiosity, a time of wit, literacy, and passion undercoated with a pervasive anxiety. Again, it's 1963, by which I mean to say that it's culturally 1958 going on 1968.

"Whoever you cast, they better be good friends." That was the post-production wisdom of the terrific young actor who originated the role of Kevin (Josh Gaboian). He's so right. The only stable thing in this play is the friendship between Kevin and Clyde. It's there in Scene One; it is still there in Scene Eighteen. That's one of the points of the story: Such bonds can exist. That fact, of course, has to be weighed against the darkness of the world.

Structurally, Clyde shifts the course of the play in Scene Seven. In fact, he simply takes over the last two scenes in each act.

Phipps: If he ran for office, he'd win. He is formidable. He is more patriotic than you are. He is right, always. He is dangerous.

Finally, a few random notes.

Apropos Scene Eleven: I once heard myself telling a director unfamiliar with the play that the funniest scene in it is the one where Darla and the boys are watching the Kennedy funeral cortege. There was an audible gasp over the phone, followed by a profound, accusatory silence. "No! No," I pleaded. "It's totally respectful!" Dial tone. If Scene Seven does what it's supposed to, Scene Eleven will work.

Scene Twelve: According to page 72, this is where you will find "Detailed notes for the staging of this scene." Sorry. I lied. You're pretty much on your own. Here are a couple tips—take them for what they're worth. The bamboo tiger cage prop has to be light, easily portable and persuasively constraining without visually obscuring Fogarty. I've said very little about music in HIGH FLIER, but I would suggest that in Scene Twelve you explore some of the gamelan music available on certain Lou Harrison albums (see Cambridge Records CRS 2560 or Composers Records CRI 455). It may not be precisely accurate ethnically, but it puts you in that world.

There's a line in Craig Lucas's RECKLESS that I've always liked. "The past is something you wake up to. It's the nightmare you wake up to every day." Scene Twelve invites you to share the nightmare Fred Fogarty wakes up to every day.

Hovering over Scene Fourteen like swamp gas is our knowledge that Lee Harvey Oswald's life is going to end right here. Only Kevin is clueless. (Well, maybe not just Kevin. One night I heard a girl behind me exclaim, "You mean he got shot on *television???*") And then, just like that, Fogarty is gone. Vanished. I wrote the play to try to figure out where.

Scene Sixteen: C I A and F B I agents infiltrated college campuses routinely during the time of this play, and university administrators facilitated it. The most recent stories regaling us with the details of this surfaced in June 2002. You may wish to refer to the A P wire service story out of San Francisco dated 6/9/02. On June 16, 2002 the New York Times editorial ("The Bad Old Days at the F B I") intoned, "These accounts of the F B I's malfeasance are a powerful reminder of how easily intelligence organizations deployed to protect freedom can become its worst enemy."

Scenes Fourteen through Seventeen pound Kevin like hammers. They assault his beliefs, his pride, his self-confidence, and his capacity to love. In truth, there's been an epistemological cancer eating at his certitudes throughout HIGH FLIER. But there is an almost personal malevolence about those four scenes as the deaths and disappearances mount. What we are watching is the erosion of Kevin's youth. He's watching it, too.

I wasn't able to persuade myself to arrive at Scene Eighteen until after the original production even though I had first toyed with the notion of a Bluebell Lake frame device as far back as May 2001. Finally, though, Clyde just took over and ended this play for me. For which I thank him.